RELEASING

A Counterintuitive Approach to Apartment Leasing

William Butler

10-10-10
Publishing

RELEASING: A Counterintuitive Approach To Apartment Leasing

Copyright © 2019 by William Butler

ISBN: 978-1-08203-530-2

Published by:
10-10-10 Publishing
Markham, Ontario

First 10-10-10 Publishing paperback edition
May 2019

Contents

Foreword   vii

A New Perspective   ix
My Vision   xiii
Hitch Theory   xviii

Chapter 1: You Had Me Before Hello   1
Hitch Leasing Principle on Preparation   1
Knowing YOUR Market   7
Underwork Your Competition   12
Fail to Prepare, Prepare to Fail   18

Chapter 2: The Perfect Wingmen   25
Hitch Leasing Principle on Staffing   25
You CAN'T Accomplish Everything You Put Your
Mind To – Be Niche   30
Relationships Outside of the Workplace   34
True Definition of Leadership   38
Myth of Motivation   43
Respect Is Not Given; It's Earned Through Discipline 49
If You Want to Accomplish Your Goals, Forget About
Them   52
You Should Pay Them to Do Their Job   56
Culture Is Cultivated, Not Created   61

Chapter 3: Laugh Now, Love Later   **67**
Hitch Leasing Principle on Outreach Marketing   67
Divorce Your EX-cuse of a Late Market   73
The Philosophy of the 10%   79
Social Media Is Key, But It's Not Everything   83
The Tabling Love/Hate Relationship   89
Self-Made Paradox   94

Chapter 4: Bag the First Date   **99**
Hitch Leasing Principle on Effective Follow-Ups   99
A System Is a Lifestyle, Not a Practice   106
Develop a Follow-Up Strategy   110
Is Mass Marketing Effective?   114

Chapter 5: Sweep Them Off Their Feet   **121**
Hitch Leasing Principle on The Tour   121
Intimacy Is Everything   125
Knowledge Is Not Power   129
Rip the Script   134

Chapter 6: S@#$ or Get Off the Pot!   **139**
Hitch Leasing Principle on Closing   139
No Means Yes, Sometimes   146
Dealing with Objections   150
Stop Selling! Start Serving!   155
Emulate Your Favorite Restaurant   162
Stressing Urgency   169

Chapter 7: All the Feels 179
Hitch Leasing Principle on Hospitality 179
The Extra Mile Wins Hearts 185
Good Hospitality = Good Review 190
Secure the Bag 195
And Then... You Ask for the Renewal 204

Chapter 8: RELEASING 211
Hitch Leasing Principle on Just Work 211

Acknowledgements 213
About the Author 223

Foreword

Do you have a dream? Do you have a goal, a vision, or an aspiration that you would like to achieve, but you can't figure out how? If you are like most people, you want more out of life, but in my opinion, simply saying that you are passionate is not enough. You have to follow up that passion with action, no matter what your passion is.

In *ReLeasing*, author William Butler shows you how you will only be stifling your own success, and the success of your team, by not taking action. His ability to take an intimidating concept like apartment leasing, in all of its complexity, and simplify it into an easily digestible, elementary level for you to seamlessly apply to your daily practice is astonishing.

There is no investment in the world you can make that returns more fulfilment than your investment in people. The success of your life, your business, and your relationships depends on the value you can provide to the people with whom you live or work.

The ideas in this book are not revolutionary; they are practical. If you choose to implement them in your daily practices, you will earn yourself a first class ticket out of the sea of sameness. ReLeasing shows you how to rise to the top, lead your market and stand proudly on the island of individuality. Open your mind, grow your perspective, and get ready to challenge conventional wisdom as you read William's counterintuitive approach to finding success.

Raymond Aaron
New York Times Bestselling Author

A New Perspective

Thank you. Not just for reading my book, although I am eternally grateful, but thank you for embodying everything that I am going to discuss in this book. Truth is, nothing I talk about in the next few chapters is going to be new, cutting edge information. Too often, we get so caught up trying to figure out what is the newest, most earth shattering ideas that can drastically change the game that we begin to neglect the things that are tried and true: the good old fashioned basics. Therefore, anything that you find in this book that strikes a nerve or really inspires you, is because it is already inside of you—you just needed a refresher. By opening this book, you have just decided to redefine your knowledge for yourself. So for that, I am saying thank you for being the visionary that aspires to not only master the art of apartment leasing, but the individual who seeks to apply this knowledge in all aspects of your life. It is because of you that I am writing this book in the first place—people like you who seek to defy all limitations, go against the grain, and shatter all student housing glass ceilings. This book is for you.

There is an old saying that says "the race is not to the swift nor is the battle to the strong…" or more contemporarily, "the race is not won to the swift but to the one who endures till the end." This idea is very simple yet extremely profound in the student housing industry, especially in regard to leasing. We live in a time where people strive for the short gain. You want everything quick, sharp, and instantly gratified, often times neglecting the degree of steadfast work that is required throughout the process. Thanks to today's technological advancements and this generation being highly influenced by social media connectivity in our mobile revolutionized world, people now have an attention span that puts us in direct competition with the goldfish. And the goldfish is winning! There was a recent study hosted by Microsoft that concluded, since the mobile phone revolution, the average attention span has dropped from about 12 seconds to about 8 seconds. The goldfish, with much notoriety, has sustained an average of about a 9-second attention span. We're in trouble.

Now, why do I tell you this? Because this represents how people today are consuming information. We have fallen accustomed to ingesting all the information we need, just as long as it fits within the 60-second duration of an Instagram video, or if you are really ambitious, tune in to IGTV to absorb the rest. Unfortunately, if you picked up this book hoping that it would follow suit, I am afraid you are sadly mistaken. If you were hoping to find a quick solution to your leasing problems, or a how-to book that will give you all the answers to wildly increasing your leasing velocity, I would be remiss if I did not advise you to stop reading now and head back to the drawing board.

Okay, I take that back; don't stop reading, because I think there is still some really great takeaways, but you get my point. This book will not be the magic leasing solution you are looking for. This leasing race will be rewarded to the person who is willing to endure through the storm of student housing, and navigate the troubled waters of apartment leasing, not to the swift who are looking for a magic pill to solve all problems.

I have found that managers often treat leasing their communities the same way 90% of Americans treat their health. Think about it. When are you most compelled to go to the hospital for a checkup? I would argue, when you feel sick or notice symptoms of distress that you cannot describe, resort to WEBMD for the answers, and scare the shit out of yourself. Then the only rational thing left to do is to go to the ER to cure your perceived terminal illness. Trust me, I have been there. Instead of making routine preventative check-ups, you wait until you are suffering and stressed. Another way to look at it is, when are you most likely to fill up your car's gas tank? Most would agree that they wait until that annoying, ever-inconvenient orange light welcomes itself to their dashboard before they start to think about finding the nearest gas station. Some will even go as far as saying, "Oh, that light means I have another 20 miles to go before I'm REALLY on empty," further deprioritizing the insidious reality that their car is running low on gas, and it doesn't become real to them until they're broken down on the shoulder of the highway, marching for miles to find the next gas station. This is how many managers look at their communities. They wait until some existential leasing crisis occurs before they choose to act. Instead of recognizing the problem in advance and addressing it head on, they wait until their leasing issue has met full maturity, and then they decide it's time to work. The only problem is that now all efforts are retroactive. The purpose of this book is to cultivate a new mentality—a mentality of the proactive, not the reactive—the mentality of those who will stop following the market average and start setting the market standards.

Now, before I go any further, if you are looking for a book about leasing, derived from scientific practice, or studies on property management deeply rooted in academia again, I would hate to disappoint. This is not a book based on any scientific research but more so a book about my philosophy; philosophy in that everything you read here is what I believe to be true based on my experience, practices, and how I have achieved much success in the student housing leasing space. Anything that I share with you is a result of trial by fire; a recipe that I was fortunate enough to develop through failing miserably, countless times, just so I could figure out the few ways to be successful. If nothing else, by the end of this book, I want you to take away just one thing. Literally, if you stop reading right after this statement, I will be 100% content. Ready? If you change your mindset, you will change your lifestyle. Change your lifestyle, and your apartment vacancy will be the least of your concerns.

Let me take this opportunity to tell you who I am and how my mindset was changed.

My Vision

In the world of leasing, I have found that perception is reality. Put simply, what we choose to focus on and apply our efforts toward achieving, will invariably come to pass. Tony Robbins, *American author, entrepreneur, philanthropist and life coach,* uses a very insightful analogy to describe this idea, in one of his leadership seminars discussing focus. This theory posed the question: What if we were to see our lives through the scope of a camera lens? No panoramic view—just a standard camera lens—and whatever we chose to focus on dictates our perception. Imagine if you walked into a party and all you could see is what falls within your 12 megapixel scope of reality. Imagine if you were to focus on a pair of knuckleheads at each other's throats all night. Imagine if their once verbal dispute escalated into a full-on fist fight—chairs flying, glass shattering, screams from onlookers, going blow for blow— until the cops knock the door down, break up the fight, and everyone scurries away. You would leave with the impression that it was a pretty intense party! On the contrary, what if at that same party you chose to focus on a couple in the corner, passionately making out, with undivided attention to one another. There is no one else in the room, just the two of them, connected, and sensationally exchanging energy. You might leave, saying,

"WOW, that party was passionate!" You may even leave with the impression that everyone must have had a really good time! Interestingly, this is the same party, just different perspectives from either side of the room. You see, what we choose to focus on becomes how we perceive the world around us. Therefore, these experiences dictate what you believe to be truth; and if all you know, is all you know naturally, you will generalize that reality to be true for everyone. I mean, how could it not be? If it's true for you, it must be true for everyone else, right?

Recently, I experienced a very eye opening encounter with how I perceived my reality. I mean that quite literally. However, in order to provide context to this story, I would have to date way back to when I was just a 10-year-old, 4-eyed kid in the 4th grade at Cooper Elementary School, in West Seattle, WA. I was just a young boy trying to figure the world out. My eyes were set on what I thought to be the most beautiful 4th grader in the world, and on this particular day, the attraction was mutual. All day, we were in tune with one another. It was childhood flirtation at its finest: from poking each other just to get the other's attention, to hitting and running away, which everyone knows was the best pick up line in elementary school. We were on cloud nine! Until the recess bell sounded, calling us back in to what seemed like solitary confinement. The teacher's aide herded all of us together in a single file line to wait until our instructor came to take us back to class. She and I were separated by at least 10 kids, which proved to be equivalent to miles apart, in my mind. So I came up with the genius idea to signal her to the back of the line with me, and of course, she complied. We laughed, giggled, and in the purest use of the phrase, were playing grab ass. Slowly fading behind the now moving line, my teacher caught us in the act and sentenced us to in-house detention.

When I got home that day, it wasn't long before my actions caught up to me. I was upstairs listening to my favorite album at the time, *Welcome II Nextasy*, by Next. My favorite song, "Wifey," on track 3 of the album, was blasting through the stereo when I heard a slam echo through the air as my auntie hung up the phone, followed by a piercing yell of my full name, summoning me down the stairs. Now, everyone knows there is nothing more tormenting than when your parents call out your full name in that *"you're in trouble"* voice. I raced to answer her call. As I ran to the staircase, the only thing on my mind was, *"Please, don't let her know about what happened at school today!"* Repeating this over and over in my head, I made it to the staircase and started to decline toward my demise. Frantically racing down the stairs, I suddenly felt my feet give out from under me, propelling me into a series of full summersaults, to the bottom of the stairwell. When I hit the last step, I quickly looked up, everything in slow motion now, only to find my glasses frisbeeing through the air and crashing as they met the pavement of the backyard patio. One lens completely shattered, and the other cracked beyond repair. I heard my auntie's faint voice in the distance: "See, Karma hit you before I even needed to!"

It would be another 18 years before I wore glasses again. It wasn't until I was driving up the highway, struggling to read a billboard sign, that I realized that maybe I should get my eyes checked out. I mean, what the hell, I pay for benefits anyway, so why not use them? Fearful of the diagnosis, I went to my previously scheduled appointment, only to hear what I already knew. My vision was shot. After my examination, the optometrist came into the room with a look of concern on his face. "That bad, huh?" I nonchalantly asked. The doctor said, "Bad is an understatement." He went further to explain that I have an astigmatism in both eyes, and he didn't know how I was able to read on my own, let alone how I was able to pass my driver's license exam. He was appalled by how well I was functioning without glasses for all these years.

He then wrote me a prescription that I was able to take and redeem for the perfect set of glasses, tailor made for my eyes. When I received these glasses, all at once I felt this feeling of deceit cloud my mind. Have I been lied to for the last 18 years? Everything was much clearer now. I used to hate watching Blu- ray movies and 4K televisions because I felt like they were not a true representation of how the real world looked. I used to hate taking pictures on my Samsung Galaxy Note because, in my mind, the picture quality far exceeded reality. It wasn't until that very moment that I realized everything I knew up to that point had been seen through a 720P scope. But now, with my new lenses, I see the world in 4K.

I tell you that story so you can better understand the purpose of this book. My intent is not to change how you operate your office, nor do I want to completely rewrite your training manual on how you train your team. My sole purpose of this book is to take the role of your leasing optometrist and provide a new, counterintuitive approach to how you perceive the concept of leasing, to provide another way to look at how you operate on a daily basis. Much like the story aforementioned, when we practice things for so long, we get comfortable with how they operate. Naturally, we become victims of such habit. Like they say, if it ain't broke, don't fix it, right? I disagree. More eloquently put, in an axiom by Benjamin Franklin, *"An ounce of prevention is worth a pound of cure."* Instead of waiting for your methods to prove unsuccessful before reevaluating, why not open your eyes to new proactive ideas that can prevent such failure before it comes to pass? One of my favorite books, *The Go-Giver*, reads: "The glorious irony of creation tucks its greatest truths carefully inside of paradoxes." I aim to help dissect some of those paradoxes we find in apartment leasing. Rethink the way you market, rework the way you motivate your staff, and release yourself from the conventional ways of thinking about apartment leasing. I implore you: Instead of following the path that is popular—tried and true—go where there is no path, and blaze a trail.

Hitch Theory

I remember it like yesterday. It was arguably the most definitive moment in my property management career. It was October 15, 2017, the day I was presented the Lease-up Specialist of the Year Award, from the the largest third party student housing management company in the nation. It was during the welcoming convocation at our annual General Manager Conference. The Senior Vice President of Operations, the Vice President of Lease-Up Marketing, and the Regional Lease-Up Specialist all gathered on stage to deliver a speech about the (still anonymous at the time) recipient of this award. Everyone in the audience silenced at this moment as the three on stage took turns verbally etching my name in what seemed to be the company's leasing hall of fame. Then, after arguably the best award introductory speech ever given, the presenters called out my name, and all at once, the crowd roared with applause! A standing ovation from over 300 of the company's leading employees, pictures being taken, the owners and executive officers of the company going out of their way to shake my hand—it was the closest I had ever felt to stardom in my life!

Soon after, I had been promoted to the regional marketing team, and then transferred positons to help charter the Leasing and Training division, as the corporate Training Developer. At this point in my career, I had the opportunity meet, train, and influence many different managers in just about every region in the United States.

In this experience, I am constantly asked by aspiring managers how I have met such success: How was I able to deploy to a community with a tarnished reputation, poor leasing staff, terrifyingly low current occupancy, and even worse pre-lease, and completely turn it around, leasing it to 94% in my first 6 months in property management? Then, the following year, turn around and not only lease that community to 100% for the first time in history, but repeat such success for two consecutive years to follow? How was I able to lease up two new development properties to 100% occupancy, one in Michigan and one in California, both within the same leasing year? How was I able to go into an untrained market, introduce purpose built student housing while leasing out of random coffee shops and library study rooms for months before having a leasing office, and still manage to consistently outpace the market by at least 10%, with a property almost 5 times the size of direct competitors?

Whenever I am training my teams and I am asked these questions, I give them the same answer. Don't allow these numbers to impress you; allow them to impress upon you that if you change the way you think about leasing, you will change the results you are getting. If you want to increase your velocity, stop looking at leasing like everyone else. If you do what everyone else does, you will get what everyone else gets. Be the anomaly. Start thinking about leasing like you think about dating. I would like to echo that same advice to you: Stop looking at leasing like leasing, and start looking at it as you look at the dating process. You see, in dating, you can't just up and meet someone at a bar, ask for their name, and in the same breath, drop to one knee to ask for their hand in marriage. I mean, you can, but I'm willing to bet it's not going to play out too well for you. Instead, much like leasing, there is a process to dating that oftentimes requires romance and tender love and care before really sealing the deal. But don't just take it from me: Who better to teach us about dating than the Date Doctor himself? Hitch.

Hitch is the 2005 film, starring Will Smith, who plays the dating coach, Alex "Hitch" Hitchens, as he mentors Albert Brennaman (Kevin James) to win the heart of the glamourous Allegra Cole (Amber Valletta), using a designed set of dating principles. Hitch designed these principles after suffering the devastating loss of his first love and college sweetheart in infidelity. Scarred and betrayed, Hitch vowed to use this pain to educate his fellow man so they would never have to meet the same fate. Hitch's philosophy is that no woman wakes up saying, "Gosh, I really hope I don't get swept off my feet today." Now, she might object by saying, "This is a really bad time for me," or even, "I am really into my career right now." Hitch explains that luckily, much like all of us, even a beautiful woman doesn't know what she wants until she sees it. Basic principle: "Any man can sweep any woman off her feet; you just need the right broom." I will echo this in relation to apartment leasing. A lead may object, saying, "Oh, I am just shopping around, and I'm not ready to make a decision yet," or, "I am just weighing out my options."

Truth is, no one really likes the apartment search; they like the find, and most of all, they value their time. We all know we want that x-factor that will make our next home our best home. We just don't know what that is yet. That's where I come in. My job is to help you open your lead's eyes to realize your community is what they're looking for. I am confident that any community can close on any prospect; you just need to be able to create enough value. I aim to give you exactly that in this book, by using a strategic, practical set of leasing principles derived from the philosophy of the date doctor himself, to help romance your way to 100%.

The first principle will be one discussing how leasing starts far before a lead reaches your property. Leasing starts with your preparation, how you present yourself and how well equipped you are to weather the leasing storm well before you actually start to generate traffic. We all know, if you fail to prepare, you prepare to fail. So let's discuss how you can properly prepare yourself to take on the leasing season and stand out amongst the competition.

Enjoy, and happy leasing!

CHAPTER 1

You Had Me Before Hello

Hitch Leasing Principle on Preparation

"Meditate on the image of an iceberg."

Your property is gorgeous, at least theoretically. When your community was first established, it is likely that you paid a full-service, multifamily housing interior designer top dollar to make it that way. Maybe your community has recently gone through a remodel, and you have completely contemporized everything about it. From the beautiful vinyl-plank flooring and luxury stone countertops in units, to the state of the art fitness equipment and the fully loaded business centers in the clubhouse, your property is dazzling! This property can probably sell itself, right?

The only problem is that all of your competition with even remotely similar innovations in their community are boasting the same thing: Their community can also sell itself. It is likely that in effort to maintain their competitive nature, your direct competition has gone out and upgraded their clubhouse amenities, and remodeled their units too, just to stay in line with the market. The only issue is that what was initially intended to offer a "WOW" first impression, is now more of the standard in the market. Everyone is doing it, which essentially makes your intended game changing amenities equal to white noise. Yet for some reason, still consumed by narcissism, you still believe that your amenities reign superior to everyone else's, and once your leads see your amazing upgrades, they will surely choose your property over the rest. The question is, if you have the exact same innovations as everyone else, or even less because your property is a little older than the newer supply, what makes you so confident that your amenities will outshine the rest, in the consumer's eye?

How do you distinguish yourself from every other comp in the market? How do you really create that *wow* factor that leaves a lasting impression on your leads? I cannot think of a better way to articulate this than referring to the advice Hitch gave Albert when coaching him for his first date with Allegra. The following advice introduces our first Hitch Leasing Principle: Meditate on the image of an iceberg.

HITCH: *Tonight, I want you to meditate on the image of an iceberg. Do you know why I want you to do that?*

ALBERT: *Because I'm cool?*

HITCH: *No.*

ALBERT: *I know, I'm not.*

HITCH: *I'm saying that you are an iceberg, in that over 90 percent of your mass is below the surface.*

ALBERT: *I know, I'm heavy... I am.*

HITCH: *I'm talking about who you are. It's a metaphor. Accounting, business, all of that is just a small part of a much deeper, richer Albert.*

If 90 percent of your property's mass lies below the surface, all the innovations you are adding, and concessions you are giving away, only make up about 10% of what we have to offer. The value you associate to your property, the experience you create for your lead, the customer service, hospitality, etc., is all part of a much deeper, richer part of your community. If you are leasing under the philosophy that your "property can sell itself," you are basing about 90% of your sells on only 10% of your value! With the mindset that pretty amenities and luxury appliances are all you need to lease your community, you are cutting yourself off at the knees.

Instead, emulate that of a retail clothing store in a mall. Think about your favorite clothing retailer. How do they distinguish themselves amongst the 26 other clothing stores, in a 50-foot radius (and that's just in that quarter of the mall)? Even before you walk in, what do they do?

My clothing retailer of choice is Express. No matter why I come to the mall, whether involuntarily or with full intention, I always walk by to see what they have to offer. Why? The signage outside the store makes it nearly impossible to avoid. The signs always have some captivating tagline that I feel is speaking directly to me, calling my name. Then, as signage casts the bait, the variety of mannequins dressed in the latest seasonal fashion trends hook me, and the compelling yet vague enough to grab my attention, buy one get one free, or 40% off everything, special signage, reels me in. Once inside, I am surrounded by an almost overwhelming amount of options; so much so that I don't know where to start. It's not until I see those familiar mannequin faces, dressed for just about any occasion thinkable, guiding me to the genre of clothing best fit for my upcoming event or current need, that my once scattered mind is put at ease. Anything from jeans, tee shirts, and canvas shoes, perfect for a casual walk in the park, to three-piece suits to stand out at your buddy's wedding—Express has it all. Then, just when I start to feel insecure about what color combinations will go together, I look up and see a staged shirt and tie combination that goes perfectly, or a sweater and jeans combo that is flawless. Then, to justify how well it looks, I noticed employees in-store wearing only the products bought from Express, and stock photos of models wearing identical products, allowing me to picture myself in my newly purchased outfits.

When I am training my team, this is the approach I encourage them to take. Presentation is key, and it is often the small details that make a huge impact. Having signage outside your property to drive organic traffic is pivotal. However, you can't just use any signage; it must be something with compelling content that speaks to your target audience. Then, when you get their attention, much like Express, dress your property to the seasons. If it is fall, your lead should be able to enter your property and enjoy the beautiful array of colorful leaves dressing the trees that are complimented by well-kept, beautiful grounds. They then should walk in to your clubhouse and be welcomed by the smell of Apple Pumpkin Spice fragrances in the air. They should see the autumn leaf décor and earth tone colors radiating through your property. You should have cliff-hanger signage throughout your community, discussing the amazing limited time special you have to offer. The language in this signage should be very captivating yet very vague at the same time, allowing you to save your special for your sales pitch at the end. You should always have a staged model, decorated to fit your target audience, and customized toward their interest. Imagine the journey of the college student, and decorate your model to demonstrate all occasions that the student may utilize their apartment for. If you are a student housing community targeting a specific university in your market, then have relevant university paraphernalia throughout your model. If you're targeting the business class, maybe stage an office area for working from home. Make sure every room in the model is casting an experience of someone actually living there. You may say, "Well, people in this market want to see exactly what they are getting, so we don't stage the units." Which is true in some cases, but more importantly, and relevant to ALL cases, is that your prospect is interested in picturing themselves living in your community. It is up to you to paint that picture, not show them what a full-size bed looks like.

You see your community just about every day, coming and going from work. For you, this is an everyday occurrence, and a lot of these things may seem trivial, or they become very easy to overlook in your regular routine. However, for your leads who likely will be seeing your community for the very first time, these are the things that will wow them. These are the things that matter. This is how you show off your other 90%, and distinguish your property from the rest!

You will never get another leasing day back! So put your best foot forward now to guarantee your success later.

Knowing YOUR Market

The Art of War, arguably one of the greatest business development reads I have consumed, has a very profound and popular revelation that echoes through the property management space when it comes to knowing your market:

"If you know the enemy, and you know yourself, you need not fear the result of a hundred battles. If you know yourself but not the enemy, for every victory you gain, you will also suffer defeat. If you know neither the enemy nor yourself, you will succumb in every battle." – Sun Tzu, *The Art of War*

Let's take a moment to dissect what Sun Tzu most eloquently said, but relate it to leasing our communities. Let's look at this statement in reverse, and then work our way to the top.

I think the majority would agree that *"if you know neither the enemy nor yourself, you will succumb in every battle."* You cannot go into any leasing season, blind. Product knowledge is essential to any type of sales; and especially when every conversation you are having with a lead is one where you are advising them to make at least a 12-month commitment with you, you should at least be able to answer their basic level questions about your property. Also, if you know nothing about your competition, how can you expect to beat them in any aspect, or make informed decisions that can impact your competiveness in your market? Merely blind faith in your property alone will surely lead to your demise.

"If you know yourself but not the enemy, for every victory you gain, you will also suffer defeat." Knowing yourself but not your comps, is progress, but it's not everything. To know yourself but not your competition, you will never put yourself in a position to get ahead. How do you outwork what you don't know? It's simple: You know everything about what you do know, and nothing about what you don't. Yes, it is possible that by being an expert on your property, you will win some victories; however, these small wins will never amount to the true potential you will meet by also knowing how you compare to your competition. You will never afford yourself the leverage necessary to make a quantum leap on your competition, because you don't know who they are and what they are doing. Nor are you affording yourself the opportunity to understand why some of the market share has chosen to live at their community over yours—because, let's be honest, you won't get everyone. The least you can do is figure out why you lost, so you can avoid future losses. What makes great leaders great is the ability to not only analyze what's happening now but also foresee dangers in the future, and deploy preventative action now to minimize said risks.

"If you know the enemy and you know yourself, you need not fear the result of a hundred battles." It's simple: Know your competition as you know yourself, and they can never beat you. You will always be one step ahead of them because you know their every move. You know what major incentives they have right now, and you can easily predict

what they will be rolling out in the future. And even if you don't know exactly what they will roll out, based on historical data, you will know when they typically approve incentives, and how they are going to market them. You know what new amenities or renovations they are bringing into the market. You know how late their clubhouse stays open, and how long their shuttle runs. You know exactly how pre-leased they were last week compared to this week, and their current occupancy. How can you possibly lose when you know everything about your competition, right? In my experience, this is the culture that rules the apartment leasing community. This is what we live by; however, somewhere along the line, we may have misinterpreted this lesson.

The leasing culture we live in has conditioned you to learn everything about your competition to determine your success in that market. You are trained to shop your competition weekly to figure out their rates and specials; thus, determining your incentives so you can remain competitive in the market. So, naturally, you stalk all social media platforms to learn what your comps are posting that is getting the most engagement, or review what ads they are running, to review their specials. Then, if you recognize that they are finding success, you emulate that on your social media, hoping to get the same results. Similarly, you focus on how late your competition operates their amenities, and how much their residents utilize that luxury; thus, determining how late you will allow your amenities to operate. This ambition to know the comps in your market has driven you to almost become obsessed with knowing their every move.

Now, please, don't misconstrue what I am saying, knowing your market is great in the sense that you know everything about your competition and have the knowledge necessary to make intelligent, strategic decisions. However, if you spend all of your time doing what they're doing, where does this allow space for you to define your community's identity? Essentially, you are becoming the same property as your competition, just with a different scheme of paint. How will you distinguish yourself from the market if you are simply a mirror image of it? If you constantly do what others are doing, you will always be a follower. If you are always following, how will you ever lead the market?

In order to be the true leader in your market, you must break away from the market standard. In order to be crowned the distinguished property, it requires extractions from everyone else. Sometimes distinction comes in the absence of other's acceptance, but you must be willing to be the best in the market at the expense of losing other managers' approval. Think about it: Why do you do market surveys every week, and get shocked when your competition had a huge leasing week and you didn't? Why is it that the very next thing that you do is make an excuse to rationalize why they are out performing you? "Oh, it's because of their location," or, "It's because they just rolled out a huge leasing incentive." This is because nobody wants to see their counterparts outshine them. No manager wants to see you more successful than they are. More importantly, no manager wants to face the wrath of their clients or property owner coming down on them because someone else in the market is signing leases and they're not. This is the case for you, just like it is the case for your comps. So, if this is the case, why spend time trying to gain approval from others who do not want to see you succeed in the first place?

To lead the market, you must stop following the paths set by the market. Leaders don't follow paths; they create them. Please understand that I believe it is invaluable to learn about your market and all of your competition before starting your leasing season. It is equally important to continue to learn about your market as the year develops, to create an advantage for your property. What you need to avoid is the inevitable obsession that comes along with spending too much time thinking about what your comps are doing, which derails you from focusing on what you are doing.

Having information about your market and competition is essential to your success, but only to provide you the knowledge so you can design a plan and develop strategy as the year progresses. Conventional wisdom says that "knowledge is power." I combat that by saying it's not knowledge alone that is power, but applied knowledge that is the true power.

Utilize the knowledge that is gained from your market research to figure out how you stack up, and what you need to do to be successful. Identify your community's strengths, weaknesses, opportunities, and threats. Learn where you are more advantageous so you can control your narrative. If you are the value option, make sure you can articulate why you are, and utilize that to your advantage. If you are the brand new premiere option in the market, be exactly that! Realize that this is not going to be for everyone, and understand that some will think your rates are unreasonable. Be unreasonable! Reasonable is for the price conscious option; your job is to show value in spending a little more and getting every penny's worth. Use your knowledge to your advantage. I would like to amend Sun Tzu's philosophy with a slightly altered ideology for property managers: If you know your market, and know YOUR product, you control the narrative. If you control the narrative, you will forever control the market.

Underwork Your Competition

Conventional wisdom says, in order to be successful, you must overdo your competition. Whatever they are doing, you must find a way to one-up them; otherwise; you will not be successful in your market. If Eagle Place just rolled out a 1-month free rent concession, you have to overdo them and give away 2 months free. If Country Side is giving away a $600 signing incentive, then of course, you have to one-up them and give away a free spring-break boat cruise. Your comps are thinking the same thing. Consequently, you get caught in the infinite incentive war to gain the attention of your audience—because that's the only way a lead will choose your community over your competition, right? Another example is in social media. There's no way you can let your competition out-Instagram you. So what do you do? You follow all of comp's followers so anyone interested in their property can know about your community too. After you're done poaching all of their followers, you look at their timeline to see what they are up to: Oh, they're doing Double Tap Tuesday. The only way you can one-up them now is to do a Freeze Tag Friday, and give away an even better prize. Now the lead will surely come to your community over the competition's, right?

The problem is, following this pattern, you wind up in a never ending rat race—a fundamental vortex where you over consume yourself with what your competition is doing; so much so that you start rolling out crazy, off-the-wall incentives just to one up them, completely neglecting the group of people that you are doing it for in the first place: the students. It's fascinating the heights people will go to just to impress the very same people they can't stand. You will break the bank, buying the whole lot just to gain the good opinion of the very people you despise.

I can't think of a better example of this than my recent visit to Columbia, Missouri, where I attended the annual Fall Housing Fair at the University of Missouri. Dressing the entire lower level of the student center was about 20 respective properties, all competing for the same 400 students' attention. You can tell this was the event to show up and show out for, because everyone came looking to outdo the next. From tables with housing fair specific TV ads looping on a television display, to virtual reality stands allowing people to feel like they are physically onsite taking a tour, this place was loaded. That's not all; the amount of raffle giveaways was astonishing! There were prizes ranging from iPads, Wireless Solo Beats headphones, and Yeezy tennis shoes, all the way to a full year's free rent! If that wasn't enough, my favorite giveaway was a brand new, 2019 car! Yes, I said it—a damn car! If you visited their table instead of their competition, you would be entered into a raffle to win a car.

You stretch yourself to insane extremes to overdo your competition, just to appease people you care nothing about, who often share the same feeling about you. Then you post it on social media to create the perception that you are insanely successful, when in reality, you just blew your whole marketing budget giving away a car to a college student who would have been happy with a damn slice of pizza. You would rather lose, doing something to make your property *look* successful in the public eye of your competitors, rather than win by doing the fundamental things that work, because doing *less* may come at the cost of you being judged. Sometimes the key is not overdoing your competition but underdoing them with the basics.

There are three essential characteristics to underdoing your competition the correct way. Now, I don't want this to be taken the wrong way and used as an excuse to justify complacency. I want you to understand that underdoing your competition is an art and requires both the mentality of leadership allowing you to effectively strategize, and the ability of leadership allowing you to be technical and actually execute at high levels consistently. This does not mean to be lazier than your competition; in fact, it requires more effort.

The first essential to underdoing your competition is your ability to be humble. Humility is becoming increasingly scarce in the property management space. Everyone wants to be an overnight lease-up, but very few are willing to put in the work that is demanded to make that happen. Very few properties lease-up overnight—in fact, almost none. There may be that one unicorn property that is the only community in the market worth spending a dime on. Consequently, they accumulate a waitlist 2 years in advance, so on opening day, leases practically start signing themselves—but that doesn't happen to everyone. I wouldn't even envy those who it does happen to, because everyone knows that the only thing worse than starting with nothing is having too much at the beginning. Those property managers never have to work for their leases. So when their property inevitably starts to age, and a new supply comes online, they won't know what it's like to hustle. Being humble demands that you quiet your mind to outside judgement, and realize that it is going to take hard work to be successful in any market. There is no such thing as an elevator to 100%—you have to take the stairs, 1 lease at a time.

Secondly, sticking to the leasing fundamentals is key.

All too often, managers get caught up, leasing your property based on the opinion of others in your market; so much so that you completely neglect the basics. This is a phenomenon that Gary Vaynerchuk, *entrepreneur, author, speaker, and internet personality,* used to describe his success as his "disproportional practicality." Vaynerchuk goes further to describe that what really makes him advantageous is not some earth shattering innovation that he discovered and rolled out that changed the world, but his overwhelming ability to think more practical than his counterparts, using the basics of the already established internet as a vehicle to earn income. This is where many lack. They try to come up with the newest, most innovative form of marketing, just to grab their target audience's attention, when sometimes it's as simple as going back to square one. Instead of giving away a car to on looking prospects, realize that it doesn't really matter what you give away at your housing fair table. The majority of those students were planning on coming to your table for the free shit anyway, no matter what you were giving out.

Housing fairs are becoming more and more irrelevant each year. Students have picked up on the idea that they can get a ton of free t-shirts and other promotional items at these fairs. They go from table to table, with the biggest tote bag they can find, and literally collect as much free shit as you will give them. It's the student housing version of the game show, Shop Until You Drop, and the objective is to grab as much shit as they can, in one hour's time. Instead of putting all your money into the actual housing fair, spend just enough so you will have leverage to gain your lead's contact information. Realizing the sales statistics, half the leads don't necessarily go to the best product; they go to the salesperson who gives the first follow-up, and strategizes a plan to get their lead's attention before anyone else. Plan a big event, host a tour incentive—whatever it takes to gain their attention, do it; and do it before everyone else. Then, if you do your job here, there will be no such mention of any other competition.

Lastly, but certainly not least, you must deploy empathy. Empathy is essential and arguably the hardest to acquire of all three. This is so, because if you don't have it, you don't have it. Empathy is the ability to truly care about the well-being of your audience, over your own. Instead of mimicking your competition's social media pages, and stealing all of their followers just to give off the perception that you have a huge following, actually care about what you can do for them. What is the point of having a massive amount of followers if you're not driving any engagement? Be more focused on the content you put out, and how you can be a service to your followers, instead of calculating what they can do for your bottom line. What's in it for them? What can you do to make your lead's day better? What can you post that will make them want to continue to follow your page? What can you do to create an audience for your property, not just a bunch of dead-end followers? What can you post daily that will grab their attention, besides just your spam rate specials? Empathy is the foundation to branding your property. Empathy is the key to closing more leases. Change your perspective of how you approach your leads, and they will change theirs on how they view you.

This is how you one-up your competition, by one-downing them with the basics. Underdoing your market with your unwavering practicality is the best incentive you can offer. Your composure through the hard times, consistency with the basics, and your empathy for your people in your following is what will guide you to the finish line. If you stick to the leasing basics, you will find you don't need much more than that. Establish practicality as the foundation to your strategy, from the start, and watch the leases roll in. Then, after you're all leased up, you can listen to what your competition has to say.

Fail to Prepare, Prepare to Fail

Throughout high school, I participated in highly competitive sports—boxing, football—but my preferred sport was track and field. I remember I was in the prime of my track career, in my senior year of high school. I was one of the top sprinters for our school. I competed in the 100-meter dash, and I was the second leg of the 4x100 meter relay race. My coach was determined to have our team qualify for the state championships, so he designed a very rigorous training regimen for us daily, leading up to our weekly competitions. Every week, Monday through Thursday, he would make us warm up with a 1-mile run and a series of calisthenics to make sure we were nice and loose before actual practice. To complete this warm up, I was required to run 10, 150-meter sprints, all before I was able to begin my actual training for the day. In an effort to conceptualize this, I have to give a little more context. When I competed, the actual 100-meter dash typically lasted approximately 10–11 seconds, from start to finish. So, in preparation for this race, daily, I was required to run 1 mile, do calisthenics, and complete 10, 150- meter sprints as a warm up. That is in addition to the tailored, weightlifting training that followed the warm up daily. This workout, on average, would be at least 2–3 hours daily—just to run a 10-second race at the end of the week. At the time, I thought this man was crazy! Why all of this for a measly 10- second race? It wasn't until my career ended that I realized there was a method to my coach's madness.

After weeks of consistently beating my personal records, I eventually qualified for an invitation track meet in Bellevue, WA. This was a huge deal for me, especially now that I was being considered for a partial scholarship to college. This track meet could have meant everything, but unfortunately, I didn't understand that until it was too late. For the 2 weeks prior to the event, I played hooky on track practice. I got comfortable being the fastest on the team. I felt I was above everyone else, and when it came time to race, my complacency caught up to me. At the sound of the gun shot, starting the race, my start out of the blocks was flawless—probably one of the very best I had ever done. Then my drive was easily the strongest amongst my counterparts, which afforded me a pretty good lead from the start. My stride was better than ever, and I was clear on my way to breaking another personal record in my 100- meter dash time. Then it happened. I opened my stride to meet its full maturity and, all at once, I felt my right leg go numb. A sharp sensation climbed up my leg and radiated up my back as I fell to the ground, introducing my face to the turf. I pulled my hamstring, and in the same event, ended my track career.

When I am training my leasing team, I tell them this story to emphasize the philosophy of the athlete. As a culture, we glorify athletes because we admire their steadfast discipline. That discipline is cultivated by their willingness to submit themselves to extreme levels of strain daily, so when it comes time to compete, they are able to exert their maximum potential. Floyd Mayweather is a great example of a professional athlete that does exactly this. Mayweather, *recently retired American boxer and promoter*, holds the world record of 50 career wins and 0 losses, crowning himself as one of the most lucrative pay per view attractions and highest paid athletes of all time. When asked in an interview what he does to prepare for a fight, Mayweather confirmed that his regimen consists of at least 2 weeks of rigorous training, and 8 weeks of sparring, before competing in any professional fight. When sparring, he turns off the bell and rotates through a series of boxers, fighting each of them for 9 minutes before going to the next. Afterwards, the already fatigued Mayweather punches his way through a series of fully energized professional sparring partners, and he does punching bag drills in 30–40 minute intervals, with no rest all before his daily 8-mile run. All of this to prepare for one fight that may last 12 short, 3- minute rounds at best. When it comes to leasing, we need to emulate the mindset and the discipline of the athlete.

As community managers, you are tasked with a million and one tasks on any given day. I know, it's hard enough to find time to breathe, let alone spend time training an employee to give tours and speak eloquently on the phone. You have to deal with processing invoices to keep the lights on, collecting delinquency from your favorite residents, submitting all 17 reports due before lunch, deal with customer complaints, and the list goes on. Naturally, training an employee starts to become increasingly less and less of a priority. Consequently, leasing agent training is mostly comprised of a 1-day orientation, a few modules on fair housing and sexual harassment in the workplace, coupled with about 3 days of office fundamentals and shadowing, and then they're on their way!

The problem with this is that even your newest employee is a further extension of you as a manager and a representation of your community. When a lead comes into your community for the first time, they don't know the difference between a new employee and a seasoned one. All they know is the experience they receive in that very moment—that's it. As Hitch criticized Albert on his first date with Allegra Cole, and was caught on camera dancing out of character:

"One dance, one look, one kiss. That's all we get, Albert. Just one shot to make the difference between happily ever after and "Oh, he's just some guy I went to some thing with once."

Much like how I didn't get a second chance in my track career, by ill preparing your team from the start, you are setting them up to pull their metaphorical leasing hamstring. You don't get a second chance to make a good first impression.

I know you have a lot on your plate, but having a strong team needs to be the entrée. Create a set tour route for your leasing team. Once you are confident with your tour route, take the time to create a standardized tour assessment sheet, emphasizing all the focal points that need to be emphasized at each amenity. Now that this is already set, make sure you set the expectation that a mock tour will be assessed weekly, and a failure of the assessment can mean further consequences. The best part about having this standard is that now your team can train one another, and we all know that the best way to learn is to teach. Repeat these steps for how your teams follow up, how they outreach market, etc. Create a leasing bible of resources for your team, early, so they will forever be prepared to leave a lasting impression.

"If you fail to prepare, you prepare to fail. But if you stay ready, you no longer have to get ready,"

Your team is only as strong as your lowest performing leasing agent. So take the time to establish an A -team. Pour into your staff as early as possible, and as consistently as possible, for they are the heart and soul of your whole operation. However, there is no training in the world that can make up for a bad mindset. So, first you have to make sure you have the right people. In the next chapter, we are going to discuss exactly that: how you can go about hiring the right people, re-LEASE your team from the conventional dynamic, and cultivate the *perfect wingmen*.

CHAPTER 2

The Perfect Wingmen

Hitch Leasing Principle on Staffing

"Begin each day as if it were on purpose."

In order to cultivate a great team, you must first find the right players. How do you find the right players? You hire for them. The best managers know their current team dynamic, can identify their own limitations, and hire the right people to supplement those voids. Conventional wisdom will tell you to look for the person with the most experience. Of course, the person with the most experience is going to be the best candidate, right? Not to mention the amount of time it will save you because (let's be real) nobody really enjoys the hiring process. It can be monotonous and time consuming, and that's not even considering how long it takes to train the candidate once they are hired. If we could, we would almost always bypass the tedious vetting process of job interviews, and welcome the applicant that walks in our office with the "Perfect Candidate" sign stamped on their forehead. Unfortunately, it's not that easy. Consequently, you sought after the applicant with the most experience. You want someone who has already internalized the property management mindset, already has an understanding of the relevant skills necessary to navigate through the office, and put frankly, someone who already gets it. For that reason, we use prescreening tactics, like listing job qualifications, demanding 3–5 years' experience in leasing, 2 years in sales, 2 years of customer services, and just about any other *experience* we can think of to itemize on the job descriptions, all the while demanding they are still a student at the local university.

I agree that having some baseline level of experience is necessary, but what's the difference between hiring a leasing agent with 6 months of experience versus one with 3 years? The answer is, very little. With 6 months of experience, they've had enough time to get a good grasp on the overall idea of how things work. They have a grasp on the work load, they can speak the leasing language, and they've had enough time learn the trade secrets to good customer service: treat people like you give a shit. Most importantly, they have just enough experience to realize that they're not the most experienced, which makes them coachable. They know enough to be open minded. Newer employees have a certain level of passion and eagerness to learn; therefore, they will be more inclined to adapt to change and help you achieve your vision.

Hiring someone with ample experience can be great if you find the right candidate. However, if you're not careful, it can come back to work against you. Too much experience can come with reluctance to learn the new ways of your office, rejection to the team culture, and sometimes an opposition to new initiatives—all because of the overly played idiom, "Well, at my last company we did…" The harsh reality is that the industry of student housing is ever evolving and, as managers, you have to be flexible enough to change with it. Some people don't do well with that change, and will refuse to do so unless they find sensible advantages for themselves in it. Now you're stuck in a game of tug of war, where you impose direction just for your know-it-all employee to oppose that very direction—a classic tale of not being able to teach an old dog new tricks.

Instead of hiring the applicant with the most experience, you should instead focus more on hiring the right candidate for the job. Hire for traits like dedication to your vision, ambition to succeed in and even beyond your office, hunger, drive, intelligence, and pure hustle. This is the experience you need, not how awesome they are at organizing lease files. Hire for self-sufficiency; someone who embodies the mindset of a manager of one. If you don't assign a task list for them, they can create their own. They understand what needs to be done, and they just do it. These employees understand your vision and will go above and beyond to see it come to fruition. This level of ambition and passion that come innate in a great employee, is what inspired our second Hitch Leasing Principle: "Begin each day as if it were on purpose." These employees find purpose in what they do, each and every day. They approach each day with intent and drive. They alleviate the need for oversight and micro management; they set their own direction. Sure, the occasional redirection may be necessary, but overall, they are a go-getter; and you don't have to tell them what to do. I would implore you to adopt the hiring philosophy of the late Steve Jobs, *chairman, CEO, and co-founder of Apple,* in his theory: "It doesn't make sense to hire smart people and tell them what to do; we hire smart people so they can tell us what to do."

How do you find these smart people? My advice is to hire fast, fire faster, and hire plenty. Now, when I say *hire fast*, I don't mean just up and hire anybody off the street and give away jobs like Ellen does cars. Take your time to find the right asset to your team. Hiring someone just to wear a uniform will cost you more time, money, and stress than simply interviewing just a few more candidates until you find the right one. Until you find them, you must be willing to do the job yourself. Anything is better than hiring dead weight.

What I mean by *hire fast* is to not question your good judgement. If someone is awesome, hire them! If their availability doesn't fit your schedule, hire them anyway!

There is always room for exceptional! There is no need to keep interviewing just for the sake of formality. If they are awesome, bring them into the fold, and if your initial judgement was flawed, fire them just as fast. It's that simple. We are in the student housing industry, where turnover is inevitable, so you are going to want to over-hire anyway. If you're budgeted for 8 CAs, hire for 10. Very seldom are you going to come across a leasing year where every leasing agent on payroll works all 20 hours per week, every single week. More realistically, if you do even manage to keep all of your original hires throughout the whole leasing season, most weeks they are going to fall between 15 to 17 hours, if you're hiring students. Not to mention, when dealing with students, you have to accommodate for the inevitable time off request for dumb shit, like St. Patrick's Day or Cinco De Drinko, so they can go get wasted with their friends. So, be strategic and hire to account for this in advance. At the very least, having more bodies in the office means you have more hands on deck to help market and close more leases. We can all agree that there is always room on the payroll for that.

Lastly, ask the right questions. Let's be real; the whole greatest strengths and weaknesses thing is getting played. I can guarantee that your interviewee has been asked that same question in some variation, at just about every job interview they have had up until this point. If they haven't had a job interview before, I bet they practiced that one in their mock interview before meeting you. People can come up with a creative way to answer this question. Hell, people can come up with a creative way to answer just about any interview question. Finessing your way through an interview is easy, and I'm pretty sure, nowadays, they can even get a credit or two at their university, for BS'n a Job Interview 101. On the other hand, you cannot fake true leadership. Dive into their background and accomplishments elsewhere. How have they set the bar before, at previous positions? What are examples of goals that were set for them that they overachieved? What self-employed projects did they take on in previous employment that exponentially added value?

This is who you're looking for: the person who is willing to put their nose down and work, even when no one is watching; someone who is excited to be at work, and is making every minute count, instead of counting every minute. I am talking about the people who hustle; the people who work with purpose, on purpose. Hire for passion, inspiration, and ambition. This is who you want on your team. This is the stuff that can't be taught. Hire for exceptionality and self-sufficiency over merely experience alone. These are the qualities that will make for the perfect wingmen.

You CAN'T Accomplish Everyything You Put Your Mind To – Be Niche

There are many profound lessons you can learn from the mentality of a chef, if you pay close enough attention: from the way they market their product and create an audience, but most relevant, how they manage a team. I am not talking about each individual employee, but how they create the art of that 5-star dish we are willing to pay top dollar for. For instance, I recently found myself watching a 3-minute tutorial on Gordon Ramsay, *British chef and television personality of Hell's Kitchen, Master Chef, and more*, creating the perfect Butter Roasted Ribeye Steak with Grilled Artichoke dish. Ramsay starts by binding the ribeye in Saran wrap to properly constrain it, making it easy to slice evenly. He then takes his carving knife and slices his desired portion of meat, and dresses it with the proper seasoning. Once complete, he warms his skillet to the preferred temperature before placing the steak on the hot surface. Ramsay then uses tongs to flip the steak, allowing it to cook evenly on both sides. All the while, he uses a spoon to shovel the melted butter over the top, cooking it to perfection. Once the ribeye is finished cooking, Ramsey then takes a steak knife to slice the ribeye into bite size, ready-to-eat portions. Lastly, Ramsey moves on to grill the artichoke. He replaces the skillet with a griddle pan, and heats it to the desired temperature, and then he takes the previously prepared artichoke and grills it to finish the dish, which he describes as *"a dream come true."* Ready to serve, Ramsay takes this finished dish, presents it on a plate, and provides a fork and knife as utensils to enjoy this delicacy.

Now, despite the fact that this sounds absolutely amazing, notice the amount of keen management Ramsay possesses over all of his utensils. Ramsay could have very easily used his steak knife to both ration the steak at the beginning and to portion the ready-to-eat sizes of meat. However, knowing his utensils, he knew that the carving knife, often greater in size and having a non-serrated edge, specializes in cutting larger portions of meat like turkey, ham, or in this case, portioning out the perfect size steak. Whereas the steak knife, usually smaller in nature and having a serrated edge, is used for more of a tough cut, so it would be perfect for cutting the ribeye when it is already finished cooking and ready to eat. Comparatively, Ramsay could have used the same skillet he used to cook the steak, to make the artichoke, but instead, he swapped it out for the griddle, to flawlessly grill this vegetable instead.

There were a lot of different ways this cooking session could have played out, but Ramsay, being a master chef, was able to identify the strengths and limitations of the utensils in his kitchen. This is the mentality that you need to embody as a manager of your leasing team.

We have been lied to since childhood. We have been taught that we can be anything we want to be if we work hard enough, and that if we exert enough energy toward something, surely we can achieve it. To the point, R-Kelly even believed he could fly and no one thought to question his sanity. So, naturally, managers welcome this ideology into the leasing world, and when you look at your staff struggling in a certain area, you see a slacker. You see someone who is not applying themselves to reach their full potential. Either that or they are incompetent. While in some cases you may be correct, in others it could just mean they are not applying themselves to reach YOUR definition of their full potential. I don't believe you can be anything you want to be. I can never be the next Michael Jordan, Michael Jackson, or Muhammed Ali. Those jobs are already taken. It's not in my DNA, no matter how hard I try. My philosophy is that you can't always be whatever you want to be, but you can for damn sure be the best version of *you* that you can be. As a good manager, that's all you can ask for.

Now, I say this with reservations, as there are staples that every leasing agent must have in order for your team to be successful. As a leasing agent, you must possess product knowledge and be able to intelligently answer basic level questions about the property. You must have adequate communication skills over the phone, via email, and in person to give great customer service. You have to be able to give an excellent tour of the community, and know the steps in a sales process to close the deal. These are must-have, leasing agent essentials. However, not everyone is going to be the best at managing your social media platforms. Not everyone is going to be the best at outreach marketing to large groups, or pitching group sponsorships. Not everyone is going to be good at manning the books and helping with audits. Sure, we can teach each and every employee to do every job, much like Gordon Ramsay could have used a fork to shovel the butter over the steak. If he worked hard enough, maybe it would have worked; but let's face it, the fork just wasn't the best fit for the job.

Find your strengths in your office. If you have an expert in outreach, who loves talking to people, why cage them behind a desk making lease files instead of driving traffic to your community? If you have someone who is very operational-minded and works well with numbers, but not so well with groups, why force them to go to the next sorority chapter meeting to pitch a partnership? Realize the strengths of your team, and play to them. Stop submitting your players to perform in foreign territory; instead, position them to win by always having home field advantage.

But in order to do that, you must first know your team.

Relationships Outside of the Workplace

In order to be a great leader of any team, you must first seek to be a mentor. What does it mean to be a mentor? According to John Maxwell, *American author and speaker with primary focus on leadership,* the definition of mentorship is "the transferal of wisdom extracted through experience." *Experience* meaning something you know and have lived through. You can't take someone somewhere that you yourself have never been, just like you can't teach lessons you've never lived. You may converse about it, but to truly be a mentor, you have to have lived the lessons you teach. Thus, Maxwell explains mentorship as being both a noun and a verb. It is something you do, something you are, and something you aim to pour into others with the intent to see them grow.

I remember my first encounter with mentorship. It was my junior year of high school when I met who I thought was just my math teacher. Little did I know, not only was he shaping my mind but he was shaping my life. For the sake of anonymity, we will call him Patrick. Patrick and I developed a really fruitful teacher-student relationship, as I was, as he described, "one of [his] brightest." Not that I was exponentially smarter than anyone else, but my intelligence, coupled with good attitude, was a pleasantry. However, Patrick came into what was arguably one of the most trying times of my life. This was the year my oldest brother, younger sister, and I were given notice that we were going to be evicted from our apartment. Dealing with this reality, my brother, taking on his position as the oldest, sought to find us a house to rent so we could avoid being separated. Unfortunately, instead of finding a house in his search, he found out that he had terminal colon cancer. We were kicked out of our apartment, kicked out of a temporary living arrangement after my brother's passing, and separated, which is exactly what we tried to prevent in the beginning. Murphy's Law was in full effect because, literally, anything bad that could happen, was happening all at once. However, as a high school student with a reputation to uphold, I had to maintain my poker face.

I would attend school as upbeat as usual, but now with a temper fuse much shorter than before. Sometimes I would have to leave class to avoid anyone noticing my occasional breakdowns, but Patrick saw past the bullshit. He recognized my potential spiraling down a rabbit hole, beyond a point of no return: grades plummeting, frequent tardiness, acting out in class, and the list goes on. Where many other teachers would have wrote me a disciplinary action form, Patrick stepped up and took me under his wing. Not knowing a single person besides me, he volunteered to escort me to my brother's funeral, knowing I had very minimal external support, and otherwise could have missed the event. He would stay after class, after hours, to provide extra time, assistance, and a positive space for me to finish my homework. When I would meet certain milestones, whether school related or personal, he would treat me to a meal outside of the class to talk about goals and aspiration, even beyond my math work. I still remember one of the more profound lessons he coached me on when I apprehensively contemplated leaving Seattle to go to college. He told me that everything in Seattle was going to try to interfere with me accomplishing my dreams: my sister, and my ambition to always protect her; the most seemingly profound relationships I had that would eventual prove to be temporary; temptation from the opposite sex; etc. *"Everything is going to seem like it's more of a priority at first, but you are going to have to be willing to take a step back, detach, and sacrifice in order to make your dreams a reality."*

Patrick was, and still is, the definition of a true mentor. Conventional wisdom tells us that we are not supposed to associate with our staff outside of the workplace. It is frowned upon to develop any sort of relationship beyond the new leads generated and leases signed. Hell, many teachers may look at Patrick wrong for taking me out to eat to celebrate my successes and mentoring me on life outside of math. But how can you truly expect to teach, mentor, or manage someone if you don't know who they are? How can you motivate anyone if you don't know their interests, disinterests, or mental state? How can you truly make an impact on someone's life without knowing their *why*? I would argue that you can't; it's impossible. You train your staff to leave any exterior problems at the door, and never make time for them outside the office in fear of breaching an employee/employer relationship, so where is there room to really figure out what is going on in their mind?

Leadership and mentorship is about relationships. It's not top down; it is side by side. Now, please understand there is a vast difference between friendships and relationships. Friendships are mostly comprised of encouragement, whereas relationships are built on empowerment. Relationships are built on reciprocity, and subsequently, so is mentorship—reciprocity in the sense that the more you mentor someone, the more you learn as well. As Maxwell says, "The more you know, the more you know you don't know." With each lesson you teach, the further you define what you know. You strengthen your knowledge on said topic, and you learn more about your employees simultaneously.

The greatest joy I have found, working in property management, has been seeing my former employees who I once mentored, excel in their career. The countless people

I have trained and got to know outside the office, I have been able to extract their talents in a way that worked for them, and empowered them to be successful. Their success would equal my success, as we all had a common goal. Leadership is not about making carbon copies of yourself in the office and hoping that they will stick around forever. It is about planting seeds inside each member of your team, nourishing their curiosity, and allowing them to sprout into the leader they are meant to be, whether that be growing with your company or going off to start their own. It's about empathy. I encourage you to defy conventional wisdom, take your team out, have a drink off the clock if you want, and invite them over for dinner. Do whatever it takes to build a relationship with your team, because you can't plant a seed if you don't know the soil.

True Definition of Leadership

Everyone wants to be the manager. Being the manager means you're the top dog, head honcho; you are in charge. Everyone looks up to the manager because they have all the answers. If something goes wrong, the manager has the solution. If something is broken, the manager can fix it. The manager knows all, and since they know everything, they make the rules. To be a manager, you have to be strong and without weakness. You maintain a level distance and low engagement with your employees to foster respect. As the manager, everyone needs to know you mean business. Managers are not to be messed with. It's your way or the highway! At least, historically, that's what we have been taught to believe. But times are changing.

The truth is, being a manager is easy. Managers are arrogant. They have an inherent narcissism to them that they mask as self-confidence to ensure a level of control over everything. They are known to provide short-term solutions to problems, even if that means hindering the office morale and leaving a trail of destruction. Managers are entitled as well as consumed with titles and status symbols. They focus primarily on self-promotion, even if that means at the expense of their subordinates. Managers Thrive off of intimidation and threats as the motivation in their office. Because, "if you don't do your job, there is someone out there who will." To a manager, everyone is expendable but themselves. Managers will often say that the turnover rate is high because they can't seem to find good talent; when in fact, it's just impossible to sustain a strong team when your culture is built on the foundation of tyranny and toxicity. In short, to be a good manager, all you have to do is be a self-centered asshole who relies on fear tactics to fuel productivity. It's easy being a manager because being negative is easy. It's not hard to displace blame and avoid taking accountability. It's not hard to be self-obsessed and believe you're always right. It's not hard to tell others to do something that you yourself wouldn't do, and then reprimand them for not doing it.

The reality is, people don't need help being negative. They don't need help feeling down about their shortcomings. They don't need help being unmotivated.

That is all easy. What's hard is being inspired, disciplined, and encouraged to meet your true potential! That is what people need help with. This is what good employees are looking for when they join your team. Employees join companies hoping to follow great leaders; they leave because they find bad managers. Being a manager is easy. Anyone can light a fire under an employee's ass. What is hard is lighting a fire within your employee's heart, as big as the Olympic flame, and figuring out what drives them, and using that to benefit your common interest. What's hard is motivating your team to work hard, even when you're not looking, because they believe in your vision, not cowering under your order. Management is easy; being a leader—that's difficult.

Simon Sinek said, *"Leadership is not about being in charge. Leadership is about taking care of those in your charge."* Leadership can be defined as a lot of things, but if there is one thing that all leaders are, it is *humble.* Leaders recognize that true leadership is not about self-promotion but more so about the production of leaders. Leaders are selfless and seek opportunity to pour more and more knowledge into their team to allow them to grow. As a leader, you envision yourself as the manufacturer of what will become a top selling product. A manufacturer understands that their product must be successful, because if it's not, it is a direct representation of their company. They will go above and beyond to assure the product meets a certain level of expectation, and just in case it falls short, the manufacturer will always couple the product with a warranty or rebate to insure the consumer's satisfaction. The warranty is not really for the consumer; it is for the manufacturer to have a second chance to please the customer. This is how you must see your leasing consultants. Look at them as a further extension of yourself and how you manage your office. As a leader, it should be your #1 priority to make sure that your team is well equipped with all the necessary skills to be successful. If you don't invest in them, you're not investing in your vision. When a customer comes in to tour your property, they don't know that it is your employee's first week working. All they know is the impression they are left with after they leave your community. Unfortunately, there is no warranty on a bad tour; all you can hope for is that they leave a review, and you get a chance to save face for future leads.

A leader leads through servantship. The bible reads: *"The greatest among you will be your servant,"* meaning a leader understands that no one is above doing the work. They recognize that aimless delegation makes them dead weight. There is a difference between delegating to your leasing consultant's strengths because they are the best for the job, and simply dumping tasks on them because you feel you're above the work. A leader knows when someone else is better for a task, and delegates accordingly. Then, once the agent does well, a true leader will publicly give credit instead of showering themselves with glorification. A leader understands that there is no such thing as a *subordinate* in the office, as the term itself is a form of belittlement. To be a *subordinate* means to be lesser than the ordinary. As a leader, you work side by side with your team. You roll up your sleeves and get dirty, right along with everyone else. You go marketing, you make follow-up calls, and you close tours. No one is above any job.

As a leader, you understand that there is more than one way to give and receive information. Sometimes an inadequate employee really means an inept manager. Betsy Allen-Manning, *behavioral expert and motivational speaker,* describes this phenomenon with her philosophy that some people have motor skills that resemble that of a Ferrari, and some of a Bentley. Ferraris have a tendency to move a lot faster and communicate through bullet points. Communication seems short and to the point, which could come off as rude to the Bentley. The Bentley, still making progress to their destination, just likes things a little calmer. When communicating, they often give more information and give more elaborate explanations. In short, people like to receive information the same way they give it. A manager may think an employee is inadequate for a position because they are slow to pick up on certain instructions. In fact, the employee may just transfer information differently than the manager does. A leader knows their team and understands how to transfer information effectively to each respective member.

There are many ways to define leadership. But if there is anything that all true leaders have, it is humility, empathy, and authenticity. *Humility* means the capability to put your team's interest before your own, to admit that you are not always right, and to be open-minded to accept constructive criticism. *Empathy* is important in the sense that leaders get to know their team and avoid generalizing. Lastly, and arguably most importantly, they are authentic. Authentic leaders nurture a culture of devotion and loyalty. Now, as a leader, it is not to say you go without turnover as an issue, because that's not true at all. However, this time, your problem will be having to replace talent that you have promoted through leadership, instead of talent you lost through bad management. Ambitious I know, but it's often the craziest of leaders that change the world.

Myth of Motivation

It was the summer of 2016, when I signed my offer letter and relocated to Allendale, Michigan, for a promotion as a Lease-up Specialist. When I touched down, I instructed my Uber driver to take me to the location of my new assignment so I could see what I was working with. As we pulled up to the construction site, my heart filled with joy, like a child in a candy store. I thought to myself, "This is my baby." A brand new development that I would be responsible for managing, literally from the ground up. As I stepped out of the Uber, and my escort pulled away, I was sure this was what Neil Armstrong felt when he first stepped onto the moon. This is where I make history. If this property were a book, I would be the author; and at this moment, every page is bare, waiting for me to write its story. As the author, it was completely up to me to either make this novel a *New York Times* best seller, or to allow it to completely bust. All responsibility was mine, and mine alone. As I came to this reality, my joy instantly turned into something else. Now, standing in the middle of the naked construction site filled with nothing but mud and construction workers, my heart felt like it jumped out of my chest, and the void was instantly replaced by terror.

What the hell is a Lease-up Specialist anyway? How am I supposed to grow this property literally from nothing? All I had was the knowledge I had acquired as a leasing manager before this, but even that property had a damn office to work out of. All I could think was, "What am I going to do?" So I did what any manager in distress would do: I cried out for help. Intending to be resourceful, I called my Regional Lease-up Specialist and asked for direction. "I am lost. Do you have some type of Lease-up Specialist in a box, or some template telling where to start? I don't know what I am doing." Having limited knowledge of the market herself, she replied, "I don't, but with your experience, you should make one yourself. I would start by making a marketing plan." Dumbfounded by the response, my motivation now plummeted 6 feet under. How was I to make a marketing plan from a market I know nothing about?

I felt lost, like being stranded on an island. Feeling hopeless, and attempting to avoid all negative thoughts, I decided I would walk around Allendale and familiarize myself with the campus. So that's what I did. I walked on campus, and what a beautiful campus it was. It was gorgeous—a moment perfect to capture on camera. So I took a picture. Instantly, I felt the need to share the picture, so I created social media pages for the property. Once our social media pages launched, now we had to generate followers. So I started by following all the major community influencers in the market, because they had the most followers. I found myself on the respective fraternity and sorority pages, only to find that they were hosting their annual *Meet the Greeks* event that week. So, naturally, I attended the event, with no business cards, flyers, or literature in hand—just with eagerness and ambition guiding me. I was able to gather contacts for future employees and potential group sponsorships. From there, the domino effect was in full motion. Everything started falling into place. I started meeting people on campus to sign leases, and meeting with groups to establish partnerships. Soon, the amount of interest generated was starting to get overwhelming, so much so that we had to call in reinforcements. This eventually led to the hiring of my right-hand man, my leasing manager, Corey, who would spearhead this lease-up journey, right alongside me. In a sense, the amount of early success we saw that year was owed, in large part, to a split decision made in a moment's time. The decision was to just do something, no matter how small, instead of waiting around stagnantly calculating how to get to the end result. I decided to just do "it." Whatever "it" was.

Mark Manson, *American self-help author and entrepreneur*, would describe this phenomenon as his "Do Something

Principle." It is the theory that action isn't just the effect of motivation, but it is also the cause of it. My Allendale experience was a direct testament that there is truth to Manson's philosophy.

Most people look at motivation as if it is some type of prerequisite to action. If you are wanting to accomplish something, and you're not motivated or inspired, you're basically S.O.L. In order to do anything, you must first experience some existential emotional charge that motivates you. Then, once you're motivated, you feel like you can move mountains, so you sprint into action. The downfall to viewing motivation like this—as some type of inebriated state—is that you begin to cripple your mind to believe you need inspiration as your crutch before you can accomplish anything.

Looking at motivation through this scope would be best comparable to how we view coffee. Think about when you need coffee the most. When your energy is at its peak, you don't need coffee. You're already going a mile per minute. It's when you're most fatigued that you look for your second wind. Many people, who don't necessarily get along with the mornings, religiously wake up and down their first cup of coffee to jumpstart their day. Some even go back for a second cup, all before noon. Once the coffee hits your bloodstream and wakes up your personality, you can almost see a whole new person awaken inside of you. You are now more efficient, more productive, more outgoing—all around, you are getting shit done—until the 2 o'clock hour kicks in and the intoxication starts to fade thin. The coffee has worn off, and it's not until your next cup that you can feel this high again. Many people develop a dependency on coffee as a source of their energy, much like some people view motivation as a source of their action. The only issue is that the false energy that comes from that coffee high is not sustainable. Much like motivation, without it, much of your action results in a failure to launch.

The truth is, in one form or another, everyone needs motivation. A daily dose of motivation is essential to be successful in anything, especially in the marathon we call the leasing season. Some may seek their motivation from books, some from motivational speakers, some from a life-altering revelation, etc. Nonetheless, wherever you get it from, it is necessary. However, if you reorient your mind, and change the way you perceive motivation, you will realize that it is always within reach. You don't need some external charge to wake you up. You can become your own source of motivation once you commit yourself to action.

Manson further describes this theory as a motivation loop. Most people only commit to action when they find a certain level of motivation. That motivation is charged by some level of emotional inspiration. Thus, in order to take any action, you must first be motivated. Manson's theory is that if we harness our reaction to action itself, we can serve as our own source of motivation. *"When the standard of success becomes merely acting, when any result is regarded as progress and important, when inspiration is seen as a reward rather than a prerequisite, we propel ourselves ahead."*

This level of motivation does not just stop at the management level. This philosophy needs to be applied top down, to every team member in the office. Motivation charges your spirit and gives you energy. Your energy as a manager is contagious. People can walk into the office and almost immediately know when you're having a good day. Comparably, they know when you are not as well. It's because your energy shifts atmospheres. It is up to you to foster the culture of your office. Use your positive energy to cultivate an office of action — a culture of motivation.

I recently went on site visits to where one of my managers told me they were ready to part ways with one of their leasing consultants. They told me this person was unmotivated, always on their phone, and never does any work. So I asked the manager what she had tasked the consultant with, and the manager replied, "Well, I tell her every day to focus on the dashboard and call our pipeline." I replied, "Okay, awesome, and what else?" The manager answered, "Well, there is so much stuff here to do, she should be able to find something." So I spent a portion of my site visit working with this employee. I showed her the goals for the office and how we hoped to achieve them, as well as her own personal leasing goals, and how she was actually leading the rest of the leasing agents, month to date. I showed her our vision, gave her tasks to help us achieve it, and it woke up her spirit. True, she very well could have found something to do on her own. But if all your boss expects out of you is to come to work daily and act as a telemarketer, getting voicemail, after voicemail, after voicemail, with no indication as to why, would you be motivated? Even a telemarketer knows the goal that they want to achieve—not just calling the dashboard. If you're not tasking your team with more than the monotonous task of calling an exhausted pipeline, they will not see your vision. If they can't see your vision, they will not be motivated to help you achieve it.

Help your team see the bigger picture. Help them to believe in your vision. Allow them to know the *why* behind their work. Give them something—literally, anything to do that will empower them. Employing your staff with even the smallest task could make the bigger ones less of a burden on you. But more importantly, it will make your employee that much more motivated and bought into your vision!

Respect Is Not Given; It's Earned Through Discipline

Every day, we make promises to ourselves; and every day, we are subjected to an internal struggle of whether or not we are going to keep those commitments. When you set your alarm clock each morning for 5:00 am, so you can jumpstart your day, that's a promise. Now, the moment you hit the snooze button and tell yourself, "Just another 5 more minutes," that's a promise broken. When you tell yourself you're going to make up your bed each morning, that's a promise. Then, when you realize you have hit your snooze button too many times, and now you're running late and have no time to make the bed, that's a promise broken. Very similarly, when you get to work, and the very first thing you do is make your laundry list of a to-do list, mapping out how you are going to have a kick-ass Monday, that's a promise. Then, when 4:45 pm comes around, and you take another look at your task list, only to realize you only checked 3 items off, that's a promise broken. The average conscious adult makes about 35,000 decisions per day. That means you have about 35,000 different commitments you make to yourself daily. How many of those commitments do you stay committed to? How many broken promises do you make to yourself? If you make so many broken promises to yourself daily, how can you expect your employee to stay true to the checklist of tasks you delegate to them?

People feel that because their title says Community Manager or Leasing Manager, they are by default entitled to the respect of their employee. You make the rules, and they have to follow them—that's just the way things work. This may work at first, but this oppressive management style has a very limited shelf life. Respect is not given by title; it is earned through discipline.

Think about the people we idolize culturally; what makes them so special? Why is it that people will camp out for days in front of Footlocker, literally kill one another for their spot in line, just to get a pair of the newest released Air Jordans on opening day? Because, despite all external distractions, Michael Jordan committed himself to becoming arguably the greatest N.B.A. athlete to live, embodying the mindset that *"you have competition every day because you set such high standards for yourself that you have to go out every day and live up to that."* Why is it that women spend top dollar and will go through hell and high water to secure the next Kylie Jenner Lip Kit? Because Jenner made beauty her life's discipline. She took her early obsession with wanting to have fuller lips, and turned her ambition into a $29 lipstick sold online, which quickly transformed into over a $420 million empire in only 18 months' time. Why is it that Colin Kapernick was chosen to feature the thirteenth anniversary "Just Do it" campaign for the globally dominant athletic apparel brand, Nike, despite his highly controversial notoriety with the N.F.L.? Because he was willing to sacrifice everything he dedicated his life to, to bring social awareness to the issue of police brutality and injustice, by taking a knee during the national anthem. As a culture, people aspire to be like Mike, have Kylie Jenner lips, and "believe in something even if it means sacrificing everything," like Kapernick. Why? The answer is, *discipline.*

It is your discipline that yields respect, not merely your title. Your team will follow you because they see you are committed to the success of your property. You don't just speak it but the pheromone of self-discipline seeps through your pores, intoxicating everyone around you. They can almost feel your commitment because it impacts your every decision—the emphasis you place on punctuality, the enthusiasm you have for outreach marketing, and the undisputed effort given on every tour to assure you close the deal. Everything you do moves in accordance to your disciplines. Your disciplines, however, are directly dictated by your vision. Dr. Myles Monroe, *Bahamian speaker and leadership consultant,* explains that sight and vision have a vast difference. Sight is your ability to see what is physically before you. Vision is your ability to look into the future at what has yet to come, and to have unwavering faith that it will come to pass. Identify what your vision is. Whether that vision is 100% occupancy, or to achieve at least a 50% resident retention rate—whatever it is—declare it as your vision. Then, once you have your vision, stay committed to it through self-discipline. Stay committed to your commitments, and you won't have to tell your team what to do. They will already be doing it out of respect for you as their leader.

If You Want to Accomplish Your Goals, Forget About Them

Jim Rohn, *American entrepreneur, author, and motivational speaker*, says, *"Discipline is the bridge between goals and accomplishment."* So, now that you have established your vision, and you understand that discipline is the key to accomplishing that, all that's left is to set your goals that will get you there.

Common knowledge will tell you that in order to accomplish your goals, all you have to do is give them your undivided attention. As long as you put your mind to it, you can attain anything. So, naturally, people do exactly that. You set some predetermined goal of 120 leases to sign this month, roll it out to your team, and practically obsess over it for the next 30 days. If your team signs 5 leases that day, great; but it's not 120 yet. The leasing agent who is off to a slow start is now stressing out because they have a goal set to sign 20 of those monthly leases, and they can't seem to close a deal for the life of them. It's mid-month now, and you're nowhere near 120 leases, so you start making justifications as to why you are not closing as many leases as you thought you were going to. You repeat these excuses to yourself, over and over again, so much so that even you start to believe them to be true. You have mentally taken yourself out of the fight, and on top of that, now even you're convinced that everyone in the market knows you give away better incentives toward the end of the leasing year, so nobody is signing now.

The problem here is not that everyone in the market has caught onto your incentive schedule. The problem is that your early obsession of your goal led to your own self destruction. You mentally defeated yourself, and then your mind did exactly what it is designed to do: protected you from feeling incompetent by giving you the bright idea to deflect the blame and place it on market conditions. To find success in anything is about 80% psychological and 20% technical. So, by losing the fight mentally, you subject your team to only about a 20% fighting chance.

It's like the 90% of America that commits to the New Year's resolution of losing weight. Let's say you want to lose 10 pounds. So, come January 1st, you plan to do everything all the health books tell you to: exercise for at least 30 minutes per day, for a minimum of 5 days a week; drink a gallon of water daily; and adopt a healthy diet. If you commit to this regimen, the fat will surely just start falling off. So, day one, you drink a full gallon of water, practically eat nothing but bird food, and you go to the gym for your 30 minutes, doing the recommended aerobic work outs. You feel so good about this accomplishment that you race to the weight scale, only to find that your weight has not changed. Slightly discouraged, you commit yourself to giving it a shot again tomorrow. Sure enough, you repeat your newly established routine: one gallon of water, 30 minutes of exercise, dieting, and then immediately racing to the weight scale. This time, you find that you actually gained 2 pounds. Feeling hopeless and outraged, you talk yourself out of this self-employed torture, and into a Chick-fil-A chicken biscuit. Just like that, you mentally defeated yourself from achieving your goal of losing 10 pounds, discouraged at the idea that you gained weight instead of losing, and not taking into account the fact that you just drank 2 gallons of water, which naturally could have contributed some water weight. You see, it wasn't the fact that the fast food market changed, or that healthier food has become less accessible; it was because you lost the battle mentally. You were too focused on your *micro goal* to see the *macro picture*.

Reggie Rivers, *motivational speaker*, eloquently said, *"If you want to achieve your goals, don't focus on them."* He goes further to say that if you focus on your goal, you will never achieve it. As the leader, you have to reorient your team's mind to stop focusing on the goal and start focusing on what is within their control: their behaviors. Your behaviors are your disciplines. Behaviors are short-term things you are doing now, tomorrow, this week, etc., which are within your control. Purposely commit to focusing on your behaviors, and you will achieve your goals. Instead of assigning your team a monthly lease goal of 120 leases, assign the team a goal of 30 leases for the week. Now that you know you have to get 30 leases this week, and have 6 leasing agents, assign each of them a weekly goal of 5 leases. Now, if you have a set closing ratio of 30%, you know that your respective leasing agents just have to go out and find at least 17 new leads that week, of whom they can invite in for a tour. With an employee that is working 5 days a week, all that means is that they have to dedicate 1 hour of their shift to finding around 3–4 new people who share even the slightest interest in your community, and if they do this, they will be on track to accomplishing their goals.

Focusing on your goals makes you incapable of seeing anything outside of that. You obsess over this huge accomplishment so much that you cannot appreciate anything other than that. You won't allow yourself to celebrate the 5 leases you signed today, because you're too focused on the 120. The problem is that everyone's battery runs out of energy at one point, and without a recharge, you will surely burn yourself out. When you focus on your behaviors, it allows you to celebrate small successes; thus, motivating yourself to keep working on the next milestone.

This motivation recharges you, your team, and your office morale. If you focus on your goals, you will never achieve them. If you focus on your behaviors, you will not only achieve your goal, you will become them. And at the end of the day, the goal itself is not what you should aim to achieve. The team you develop during the process of achieving that goal is what is most important.

You Should Pay Them to Do Their Job

If leasing your community to 100% occupancy is your destination, then that makes your current leasing team the vehicle. If your team is the vehicle, then motivation would be considered the battery. Whereas motivation may not be the whole car, it is absolutely invaluable to the success of getting you from where you are now to where you aspire to be. However, much like any battery, your motivation has a shelf life, especially if you are over exhausting your vehicle—your battery is bound to need a recharge. It's like what happens when you park your car and accidentally leave your headlights on all night. When you return to your car, the battery is completely exhausted, and your car will not move until you get a jump-start. This is exactly what will happen to your team. Just like every battery that is overworked, yours will run out of juice too, and it is not until you jump-start your motivation that you get your team up and moving again. Internal incentives are the necessary jump-starts to charge your team back into action.

It was January of 2015, when I experienced my

epiphany with the importance of incentives as a source of motivation. My little sister had a mandatory internship with the Washington State Legislature, which as an aspiring attorney, was a dream come true. However, along her journey, she came to a fork in the road, involving her son, 5 years old at the time, and his behavior at school. Troubled by the new school, new environment, and unfamiliar teachers, my nephew found himself in an endless cycle of behavior issues, which soon led to his indefinite suspension from his pre-school. My sister, distraught at the idea of having to withdraw from her internship, called me, asking for advice. Should she sacrifice this opportunity of a lifetime to fulfill her obligation as a parent, or should she try to explore other student programs that weren't as financially sound but would allow her to continue her internship? Neither were ideal, but these were the cards that were dealt. I quickly threw in the trump and volunteered to watch my nephew for the 2 months until she could finish her program.

Juggling all the responsibilities of being a leasing manager, and nurturing my nephew through his transition into another unfamiliar school, I too had an encounter with the same behavior issues that had led to his initial suspension. Quickly, I learned that we were going to have to curb his bad behavior or continue to suffer from this infinite cycle of events. So, he and I sat down one day and designed a program that worked for both of us. This was our *rock star behavior program*. For every day that he did well in school, his teachers would give him a gold star.

Once he got a star from his teacher, he would be able to add a star to his *rock star board*. Once he got 5 stars in a row, equivalent to 1 full week of good behavior, he would get a prize. Every weekly prize led up to his suggested ultimate goal: an all-inclusive trip to Xtreme Arena, a Nerf gun stadium, at the end of the month.

Knowing what his end goal was, this kid was stoked to go to school. He would listen to his teachers, help other students, and overall, be an outstanding scholar. The teacher would rave about my nephew and his new-found behavior. They would complement him on how attentive he was in class, and how much better he dealt with conflict with other students. He had a whole new perspective on things, because his focus changed. Before, he was just going to school because he had to; but now he was excited to not only go to school but to get a gold star for being a good student. Every day, after he received a star from his teacher, he would sprint to the parking lot, jump into my arms, and I would publicly lift him into the air, sit him on my shoulders, and chant his name as if he was the King of Windsor Elementary School. I remember the very day it sunk in: It was after he got all 5 stars for the week, and I treated him to a deck of Pokémon cards and ice cream, when he declared, "I like being a good kid, Uncle. I get a lot of fun stuff for being good, and I don't have to do wall-sits in time-out." Needless to say, we went to Xtreme Arena that month, and the kid earned every minute of it.

You see, my nephew had the potential inside of him all along. It wasn't the new school that dictated his success, nor was it curriculum or the teachers, for that matter. It was his decision to be a rock star instead of continuing to go down the path of the troubled student, and facing the consequences associated. What was it that woke him up to maximize his true potential? Nothing more than a little incentive. The recipe has not changed. We all need a little incentive to recharge ourselves when our battery runs thin and we're not motivated. For my 5-year-old nephew, his incentive was Xtreme Arena. For you, it may be your next job promotion, or that big bonus you get at the end of the leasing year for hitting your budgeted occupancy goal. Whatever it may be, it serves as your jump-start when your battery runs low. So, if you depend on incentives for motivation, and my 5-year-old nephew depends on incentives for motivation, why is it that we believe our young adult, leasing agents don't need an incentive for a part-time job that they are probably only using to pay off their student loans?

All too often, managers default to the idiom: "I shouldn't have to pay to do your job." You would rather give incoming prospects, that you know jack shit about, a $1,000 gift card to sign a lease with you. You will incentivize a complete stranger, but you don't want to incentivize your staff, the very people busting their ass daily to get these leads to sign in the first place. In theory, yes, your leasing agents are already getting paid the minimum wage salary you give them to work there. But your leasing agents are people too. They get excited about incentives, like all of us. Sometimes the $25 commission they receive for signing a lease just doesn't cut it. As the leader, it is your responsibility to extract the true potential in each and every one of your team members. You have to find a way to motivate and empower your team to keep moving in the direction of your vision. Giving an incentive for their work is a small investment that will yield a huge return.

Reward your team for their hard work, and publicly celebrate their success. Incentives come in many forms. It could be awarding one of your leasing agents with the *Rock Star of the Week* reward of a $25 gift card for doing a great job, or it can be as big as awarding that employee with an Xbox One, or a Sephora gift card, for signing 10 leases. Don't just limit your incentives to money. Sure, that's appealing to everybody, but that's also a cop out. Think of the things that all of your staff would want to have but may not want to spend their own money on. Because, let's face it, if you give them extra money, they're probably just going to spend it on rent, or some other boring adult obligation, like insurance or some shit. I remember the time I rewarded one of my community assistants with an Apple watch that she always wanted. She wouldn't stop raving about how much she loved her job, and her leasing numbers were living proof.

Think about your team and what really gets them going. What are their interests? What excites them? Then think about how you can use that to jump-start your vehicle. Incentivize your team, and use that momentum to propel your vehicle forward. Next stop, 100% occupancy.

Culture Is Cultivated, Not Created

Developing the culture of your office is like growing a sunflower. You can't just place a sunflower seed on the window sill and tell it to grow. Nor can you plant it in a shaded area and expect it to blossom. Growing a sunflower requires strategic timing, seed placement, and consistent nourishment. Most importantly, for a sunflower to properly blossom, it must be bathed in sunlight each day.

An office culture is not a set of policies enforced by a manager upon the employee. It's not a set of slogans or motivational quotes of the month. Culture is not your office's annual Christmas party, staff outings, or team pictures. These are events that you occasionally do. Yes, these things can contribute to your office morale, but these are not your culture. You cannot instill a culture; it cannot be created. Not to mention your employees were not born yesterday; they can pick up on it when you force an artificial culture. They know when it's not authentic. To develop a sustainable culture, you do so through consistency. Jason Fried and David Hansson, *authors and founders of 37 Signals*, said, "Culture is the by-product of consistent behavior." They go further to explain that if you reward trust, then trust will be built into your culture. Likewise, in the leasing world, if you encourage a steadfast work ethic, it will be built into your culture.

The problem with many managers is that they try to establish a culture based upon a set of preconceived precepts of what an office culture *should* be, and assume that every office must be X in order to be successful—the perfect example being the workaholic. Managers worship the workaholic. In interviews, they look for the young, eager employee with the thirst to dedicate all of their free time and energy to the job. They want someone who can stay in the office all day, completing every follow-up call, attending every marketing event, and burning the midnight oil, all just to sign the next lease. They look for employees that have the most availability and the least amount of obligations outside of work, so that they can maximize their time in the office. This is the employee that is willing to put in the double-shift, go home to sleep, and then wake up and do it again. The workaholic is glorified so much that candidates go as far as using this as a skill they list on their LinkedIn account or put on their resume before interviewing.

It is common to overvalue the workaholic because they can give us more hours. However, as Fried and Hansson said, "We don't need more hours; we need better hours." Think about the amount of time wasted in the office talking about the awesome Netflix series you just started, or about plans for the upcoming weekend. Then you turn around and put the same small talk on repeat with everyone who comes in the office that day. We don't ever get a full 8 hours out of our employees anyway, so why glorify the employee that needs more time to get the job done? We should, instead, appreciate the employee with more on their plate, who still manages to get their work done. They have mastered the art of working more efficiently, because they know they can't afford to stay after work. They have shit to do. Their sun doesn't rise and set on your property, and because of that, they know how to maximize their time spent in the office. We are too busy giving credit to the employees that waste the most time, instead of giving credit where it is due. Encourage a culture of better workers by praising the success of the smarter worker, instead of the *harder* worker, and you will begin to foster a culture built on efficiency.

Another example of a concept commonly encouraged as culture is *Casual Fridays*, which is the idea that your team has been working so hard all week that they deserve a day to relax, take a load off, and dress casually on Friday. Friday is the end of the week, one day before the weekend, and the perfect day to be a little more lax in the office, right? Many managers think that this defines the culture in their office, so they strongly encourage their staff to wear jeans and a property specific t-shirt, every Friday. If you value the importance of being comfortable and lax in the office, then why isn't this something you enforce every day? It's because you understand that it is important to always put your best foot forward. You never get a second chance at making a first impression; not to mention, the better you dress, the better you feel, and the better you feel, the better you perform. Complacency is a slippery slope. The moment your team feels like they can be laid-back in some areas, it creates a gateway to other things they will slack on. By encouraging casual Fridays, in actuality, you are encouraging the mindset that it is warranted to slack off as we get closer to the finish. You are telling your team that it is okay to mentally check out as the week comes to an end.

Interestingly, just as the week is coming to an end for you, this is also true for your prospective future residents. They are finishing up with work for the week, or they are done with school for the weekend, so now they can take care of some of the other things they have been putting off, like touring your community for example. So now they stroll into your office on a Friday, where everyone is dressed down and relaxed. Now, your leasing agents give a relaxed tour, create a relaxed experience, and give a relaxed sales pitch, all because you encourage them to have a relaxed, casual Friday.

Instead of encouraging the complacent mindset of a casual Friday, you should praise the idea of always dressing for the position you see fit for your future self. Encourage consistency in always putting your best foot forward and making a lasting impression. If you nurture a culture of the best, you will get the best out of your employees, every day, Monday through Sunday.

Culture is not something you can create. It's not something you can inject with fancy words and occasional events. Culture is something you define through consistent encouragement. Much like the sunflower, your culture will bloom where you provide the most sun. So, whatever you want your culture to be, shower it with sunshine. Reward your employees for doing a great job. Encourage smarter work, and efficiency will be built into your culture. Praise the well-presented employee on their attire, and good presentation will be built into your culture. Nurture your seeds, bathe them with sunlight, and soon, your culture will be the sunflower garden that defines your leasing office.

CHAPTER 3

Laugh Now, Love Later

Hitch Leasing Principle on Outreach Marketing

"It's all about the 'totally varied,
wildly experimental short game."

Now, if there were ever a concept in leasing that bared a striking resemblance to dating, it would be outreach marketing. Let me explain. In the early scenes of the film, there is a cameo of Hitch and one of his close friends, Ben, spending a guys' night out at what seems to be one of the more lively bars in all of Manhattan, New York. The bar was jam packed, shoulder to shoulder, with all young, good looking, white collar professionals, drinking, laughing, and partying the night away. Hitch and Ben, more casual in nature, engaged in a game of pool. Hitch, using his pool stick, guides the cue ball in to another, rocketing the secondary ball to the goal, only for it to freak in and out, which prompts the following discussion:

Ben: You know what your problem is, Hitch? You're all about the short game. You pick your shots based on what you see first, not what's necessarily best for you... in the long run.

Hitch: All of us are not married to the woman of our dreams and about to have a baby. You know, I'm very happy for you. Just not meant for everybody. So please just leave me to my hot, sweaty... totally varied, wildly experimental short game.

Ben: I was talking about pool, but whatever.

Hitch: Yeah, okay.

This conversation briefly continues before it is interrupted by the dazzling Mandy, played by Paula Patton, and her equally gorgeous counterpart, who enter the room and steal the show. Ben, losing all train of thought, hypnotized by Mandy's beauty, prompts Hitch to ask:

Hitch: Do you want me to go get them and bring them over here?

Ben: No, don't do that.

Hitch: Are you saying you don't wanna talk to them because you can't go home with them?

Ben: I'm just trying to keep my head above water.

Hitch: I'm gonna go get those girls, bring them over here... and we're gonna have a conversation like human beings. Then you're gonna go home, and I'll take them back to my apartment.

Ben: Well, that sounds like fun for me. But you might want to get in line, pal.

Hitch, letting mere confidence guide him across the bar, infiltrates the pack of drooling onlookers and, most literally, grabs Mandy's attention by the hand. The pack of outraged men all stare in jealousy as Hitch charismatically sparks a compelling conversation and courts Mandy away as planned.

You see, if leasing is like dating, then outreach marketing would be considered the pick-up line. The problem is that most managers adopt the rational mindset of Ben. As a manager, it is your innate ability to be a rational thinker. Your brain, by design, is hardwired to talk you out of situations that are risky, scary, new, or uncertain. So, naturally, you are hyper-invested in calculating the outcome of a situation to identify *what's best for you in the end.* You want to minimize the amount of risk, and maximize the amount of reward. You are so invested in the outcome that in the face of an opportunity, you often talk yourself out of anything that you are uncertain about or unfamiliar with. Notice how Ben, obviously interested in meeting the women, completely shuts down when Hitch presented the opportunity to meet them: "No, don't do that... I am just trying to keep my head above water." Ben faltered, not wanting to speak with the women, simply because he was unable to go home with them. Then, when Hitch persisted, Ben doubted his ability by saying, "You might want to get in line, pal," implying that because so many others have tried and failed, Hitch would most certainly meet the same fate.

Unfortunately, this is how many approach marketing. You see a lead, and for one reason or another, you hesitate to speak to them because you feel you are not able to seal the deal right away. You often calculate your success based on others' failure in a market. You spend your time marketing, hoping to find the leads who already have a vested interest in living in your community—the low hanging fruit that already want to sign a lease. You pick your shots based on what's best for you in the end, instead of looking at *the short game*. The harsh reality is that outreach marketing is primarily rooted in the short game. Outreach marketing is a numbers game. It's a basic game of probability: The more people you reach, the more traffic you draw, and the more traffic you draw, the more leases you sign. It's that simple. Prejudging or self-vetting leads, before their actual screening, only cuts you off at the knees. Your job is not to self-qualify your leads; that's what your resident screening process is for. Your job is to be totally varied and wildly experimental in your outreach marketing.

Instead, meditate on the mindset of Hitch. To be

effective at outreach marketing, you have to first understand that your objective is to grab the lead's attention. That is it. We just defined everything that outreach marketing is about, in one sentence: Grab your lead's attention. It's not about signing the lease right then and there. It's not about finding the person who already wants to live in your community. It is solely about day trading attention, and piquing your lead's interest. Outreach marketing is all about your self-confidence. You have to first believe that you have a great product to offer, and that you have something that distinguishes you from the rest. Use that confidence as your guide as you approach your prospect. Then, don't just pass them a flyer, or hand them a pop socket—do something that will grab their attention—no cookie cutter pick up line, or the classic, "Do you know where you're living next year?" Be original, and spark a compelling conversation. Create common ground with your lead, leaving them wanting to see you again. That's what it is all about. Too often, people get so consumed with the outcome that they forget the root of why outreach marketing is so successful in the first place.

Outreach marketing is a philosophy deeply rooted in interpersonal communication. It is the connection that one draws from a prospect when physically being present and sparking a relationship with your lead, beyond simple marketing techniques. Outreach marketing, when performed correctly, is designed to grab your lead's attention, distinguish your community from the masses, and brand your property. This small gesture can be the difference between having a *late market*, where your property hit budgeted occupancy in August, opposed to having your property leased up to 100% by the beginning of May, because you moved the needle. Outreach marketing is one of the most important things you can do to impact your leasing velocity, because it is tapping into the key component that you often lose sight of: human to human interaction.

To be successful at outreach marketing, you have to stop thinking about leasing, and start thinking about dating. Start thinking about the people we are talking to, not the outcome. When it comes to dating, there is a process to it. You don't just walk up to someone and ask them for their hand in marriage. First, you meet them, build rapport, and find common ground. Then, you go on your first date, where you decide whether or not you can see a future with them. Then, you get your friends and families involved to gain their advocacy. After that's all said and done, you make your decision to commit or not. Much like dating, this is a similar process for leasing. It's not about finding leads that already wish to commit to signing a lease. Although, in apartment leasing, we do not discriminate on one-night stands. If they want to sign a lease in 24 hours, we are all about it! However, most leases require some TLC, and that process is all about the totally varied, wildly experimental short game of outreach marketing.

Divorce Your EX-cuse of a Late Market

Stop living by the excuse that your market is a *late market*, to rationalize why you aren't signing leases yet. Stop justifying your *early market* by saying it is too late in the year, and everybody has already found their home for fall. You're better than these excuses. The conversation of early versus late markets only exist to justify the marriage between you and all of your limitations, validating why you can't find success in your respective market. There is, however, such a thing as a trained market and an untrained market. If you reside in a market where people seem to be proactive and rush to secure their housing for the next lease term, far in advance, it's because the market has been trained. The prospect in this market understands that there is limited supply of quality housing in your market to accommodate the university enrollment; thus, this increases the demand for said housing, creating an abundant amount of urgency to sign leases early. There are often contributing factors that stress this urgency, such as enrollment spikes, university residents' halls stressing students to renew early, or renewal deadlines set by surrounding apartment communities, etc. Regardless of the motivation, people are urged to sign leases in your market early—coining the term, *early market.*

In opposition, if there is no urgency for prospects to secure their housing, then they take their time in the decision process. They know there is an ample amount of housing to go around, and there is no real pressing deadline; therefore, they have the luxury of time to make their decision. Dealing with Johnny, the college student whose middle name might as well be procrastinator, you can guarantee he is going to take as much time as he can get before signing his lease. By conventional definition, this is what makes for a *late market*, or what I call a market that has yet to be trained. Whether trained or untrained, there is one thing that both markets have in common: They are both highly motivated by time. The truth is, nothing would ever get done if it weren't for the last minute. As a leasing agent, it is your job to create that *last minute*, and train your market. How do you train a market? It starts with outreach marketing.

Outreach marketing is comprised of two major components: branding and prospecting. Branding is the process involved in creating a unique name and image for your community, in the consumer's mind! With branding, your overall goal is to distinguish your property from the next, so when the time comes for your prospect to search for housing, your property is the first to come to mind. The most effective way to accomplish this is through brand consistency. Your community's brand is not defined by the amenities you offer, or by how low your rates are compared to the next. Your brand is defined by what people say about your community when you are not present.

Think about some of the most prominent brands that you know right off the top of your head. When you walk into Best Buy, and you see a pure white box, modern in design, with an image of a half-eaten apple on it, you immediately identify said item as an Apple product. If you were to be watching a commercial during the Super Bowl, and an ad pops up, consuming your screen with a cherry-red background, with white, italicized, cursive writing, you would immediate draw the connection that this is an advertisement for Coca Cola. With Nike, whether you see the *Swoosh,* or the slogan, "Just Do It," you naturally connect it with the world renowned sports apparel brand. All of these brands have accomplished branding their product through consistency. Now, because of the connection you have drawn, and the meaning you associate to these brands, when you have a need, and it comes time to buy, you will immediately turn to your most familiar products to fill that void.

This is the degree of branding you should aspire to uphold for your property as a community manager. In order to effectively market yourself, you must maintain brand consistency. When you are making flyers, keep the same flyer throughout the duration of your leasing season. Only if the message you are hoping to communicate changes, should you alter the language on the flyer. Even then, you want to keep your color scheme, theme, etc. very similar, as this is how you master brand consistency. The moment that you switch up your branding on your flyer and introduce it into the market, it's like pressing reset on all the impressions you have made in said market year to date. You want your flyers, brochures, and all other collateral to be consistent with your website, social media, paid ads, etc. Lastly, now that you have an established consistency, the single most important component of branding is distribution.

Many mangers doubt the value of giving out flyers. Often, I hear managers respond to the idea as a dead marketing strategy, and that people in their market don't respond to flyers. They simply take them and throw them away. I have also heard managers state that buying certain promotional items, just to give away, is a waste of money, and that buying t-shirts is expensive, and just giving them away to people who don't live in your community is a waste of marketing dollars. Whereas there may be some validity to this frame of thought, you are missing the bigger picture. Marketing statistics prove that as early as 10 years ago, it would have taken a consumer about 4 respective impressions with a brand before they responded to any given call to action. That means someone would have to receive a flyer from you, visit your website, get a t-shirt, and see you at a housing fair, for example, before they finally decide to come down and visit your property. However, today, given the competitive space of the marketing landscape, that number has quadrupled! That means that it requires at least 16 particular impressions before any one lead responds to your marketing calls to action.

Now, imagine working at a community that caters to a university with an enrollment of 27,500 students. Imagine trying to find that one student on 16 different occasions. This is why branding is so important! Sure, that student may not live at your community right now, but by wearing your property t-shirt, it is creating a walking billboard out of everyone wearing it, which will unconsciously contribute to the amount of impressions you cast on the 200+ students with which that student shares a lecture class, or the thousands of students they pass by, between class periods. That flyer you passed out could spark a conversation between friends, which could lead to someone else's interest in your community. Just because that lead does not sprint to your leasing office the moment you hand them a flyer, does not mean that it is a dead marketing strategy; it is just 1 of the 16 steps in your marketing process.

I agree that this still does not eliminate the issue of the late market. Whether you pass someone a flyer or give them a koozie, they are still going to respond when they feel fit. People don't buy things until they find a need. Say, for example, if your phone breaks: You go to Verizon to buy the latest iPhone. When you wear out your gym shoes and need a new pair, you go to Nike. When you are hungry, you go out and you find the nearest Chipotle. That's just how it works. However, not even the most conscious buyers know what they want until they see it. That's where prospecting comes in.

Prospecting is not about finding the people who are already wanting to sign leases at your community; because, much like when you are hungry, chances are you are going to go out and find your next meal on your own. You won't need any directing. Prospecting is about finding those consumers who don't yet know that they need what your community has to offer, until you open their eyes. Prospecting is the form of outreach marketing that is deeply rooted in interpersonal communication. The primary goal of prospecting is to have effective conversations with a captive audience, maintaining the goal of sparking interest in your community, securing contact information, and paving the way for a future follow-up. This will ultimately expedite the marketing process, and drive immediate traffic, because it puts you in control of the transaction.

Effective prospecting does not have nearly as much reach as branding; however, its value is in quality over quantity. Effective prospecting requires you to stop the lead in their tracks, and engage in a compelling conversation. Your goal is to grab your lead's attention, identify common ground, identify what is driving them, and then interest them in coming to take a look at your community. That's it. All you want to do is generate enough excitement that they will want to come visit. Use what you have, to get what you want: their attention. Then, once you have it, use it to drive traffic to your community.

Those who feel that outreach marketing is counterproductive don't lack the resources to be successful; they lack the *resourcefulness*. Branding and prospecting are both vastly different in nature but are equally invaluable to your success in training your market. You work in an industry of contingency. You cannot necessarily predict when your prospect is going to sign their lease, nor can you make them. But what you can control is time—the amount of time you put into branding, the amount of time you put into prospecting, and the amount of time you allow your lead to procrastinate. Time has a huge influence on urgency and, as I said before, it's up to you to create the *last minute*.

The Philosophy of the 10%

No matter how grueling the task, big or small, everything you have accomplished or aim to accomplish is all controlled by two things: your beliefs and your values. To accomplish any goal you set for yourself, you must inherently believe that you can achieve it. If you want to have a property that meets 100% occupancy, you must believe 100% is possible. If you want to have a resident retention rate of 50% or more, you must truly believe you can renew 50% of your community. Without a belief in your ability, you will never accomplish your goals. However, sheer belief in a vision will not work unless you do. Therefore, without values to help align your behaviors and habits with your beliefs, you will lack all directions. Values are the governing principles that encourage the way you act, feel, treat, and see the world around you. If you value outreach marketing, outreach is not just something you do to check it off the task list; it's something you train your staff to do every day with zeal, out of true enthusiasm for your community. If you value staff development, you are one who is constantly pouring wisdom into your staff regularly, to see them learn and grow. Beliefs and values govern our entire lives, and when they meet, they give birth to a thing we call *passion*. The philosophy of the 10% is entirely driven by unfaltering passion.

The philosophy of the 10% is deeply rooted in the 90/10 rule: the idea that 10% of managers find a level of success that 90% won't, because the 90% aren't willing to do the things that the 10% are. The 10% possess a certain level of unshakable passion that is almost impregnated inside of them, like a fetus to a mother, and much like a mother, the number one obligation is to protect. You are responsible for nourishing and nurturing your baby to good health. You don't have the luxury of taking days off from being pregnant; you're committed to your baby, no matter how adverse times become. When you go into your office, your baby goes with you. When you go out with your friends, your baby goes with you. You don't consume certain substances or engage in certain activities, because they will submit your fetus to a toxic environment, and thus it would put your baby's health in harm's way. Even when others can't see your baby emerging within you, it's still there. However, the longer you hold on to it, the larger it grows inside of you. Then you meet a point where you no longer can keep it a secret, and now it is big enough for a blind person to see. Finally, your baby exits the shadows of the womb, comes to the light, and reveals itself to the world. Now you and everyone else in your market can see the fruit of your labor come to fruition. Everything that you have worked tirelessly for and committed to for months, is now birthed, healthy, and beautiful for the world to admire.

This is the same level of passion and nurturing you must have to accomplish your vision of 100% occupancy. You must be non-negotiable in your beliefs, and unapologetically true to your values, because the hardest thing to overcome is when you are passionate about your goals but your values conflict with those around you. As a property manager, you innately value making everyone around you happy. Unfortunately, trying to appease everyone around you inherently will lead to you hurting the one thing you are responsible to protect: your baby. Too often, when I travel to markets, I hear managers say, "We have really good relationships with our competition in this market, and we don't want to ruin that," or, "We are all struggling to fill up in this market, so we are in this together." NEGATIVE! Subjecting your team to this "we're in this together" mentality is alcohol during your 3rd trimester. It's completely toxic to bringing your vision to life.

Your ambition to find acceptance from your peers is often a direct contradiction to your vision to succeed. You play by a set of unspoken market rules to appease the very same comps who are looking to claim the same market share you are, regardless of how it may affect you. You refuse to flyer their property, or stand out during community events, to level the playing field—and for what? So that they willingly give you leasing data for a damn marketing survey? When you're 100% *who gives a shit about the market survey?* Les Brown, *arguably one of the greatest motivational speakers of his time,* said, *"In order to be successful, you must be willing to do today what others won't do, in order to have tomorrow what others won't have,"* which means, greatness requires extraction from the group. Sometimes you must be willing to go against the grain in order to find success where others fall short. Saying "you are in the same boat" is the very essence of why you will not be successful. You refuse to distinguish yourself from the others in your market. To say you have a really good relationship with your competition, and don't want to lose their good judgement, is admirable; however, it is disregarding one key detail: They are still your competition. Anyone under such a title will not ever want to see you do better than them, no matter how nice you play, so why sacrifice your success simply to make them smile?

To accomplish a successful leasing season, you have to first adopt the mindset and the passion of the 10%. The 10% know their outcome and are relentless in accomplishing it. They understand that the success of their community is entirely weighing on their shoulders, and that there is no room for excuses or complacency. The 10% realize that their success is more than simply achieving an occupancy goal. It's about who your team becomes, and the skillset they develop in the process. Similar to a baby taking its first steps, it's not about learning to take one step, or two steps for that matter. It's about instilling the ability and confidence in your child, to walk long after that moment has passed. It's about what comes next.

The philosophy of the 10% is quite simple. Simple, yes, but not necessarily easy. It is simple in the sense that very few steps are necessary. Simply believe that your success is possible, and allow your values to be your GPS, navigating your habits and behaviors in that direction. Develop an unadulterated passion for accomplishing your goals, and be relentless in making them come true. Treat that passion like your baby, and nurture it to its best health, regardless of the disapproval of your peers. At the end of the day, remember: There is no *right way* to raise a child but to raise it to its greatest potential. Your job is not to gain the approval of your counterparts, nor is it to win the award of the most liked manager in the market. Your job is not to raise your property to meet everyone else's standards; your job is to make your community the best it can possibly be, not matter what. Once you realize that, you will gravitate from all the excuses and limitations of the 90%, and induct yourself into the 10%.

Now, start marketing like it.

Social Media Is Key, But It's Not Everything

There is a vast difference between what is earned and what is given. What is given is often seen as a hand out. Not much is required, and often times it can be associated to luck. When something is given, it usually doesn't require much work, and because of that, you don't have much control over the outcome. On the contrary, for something that is earned, there is a certain degree of work that is required as a prerequisite to obtaining your reward. The reward received is inherently measured by the quality of your performance. Thus, as the earner, you have significantly more power over your outcome and the level of your success. In other words, you can't honestly say you have earned anything without first busting your ass and putting in the work to deserve it. In college, I had a very real experience that opened my eyes to the concept of what is earned versus what is given.

As a young frat boy in his early 20s, with the testosterone of a bull, working out became almost an addiction. One summer, every day, my fraternity brother and I would go to the university fitness center, have our pre-work out drink, and do a warm up until we were drenched in sweat, before we began our work out. Faithfully, at least 5 days a week, we would stay true to our regimen. We would do our routine warm up workouts before we indulged in a high intensity exercise we called 9 *hundreds*. We would pick 3 muscle groups for the day, do 3 different workouts for each, and complete a circuit workout of 10 sets of 10 reps for each respective exercise. This was our routine for at least 6 weeks straight, until one day we decided to do something different.

We decided we wanted to switch things up and shock our muscles, so one day we decided to lift heavier weight. Weighing just over 195 pounds, I challenged myself to bench press 295. Never lifting such weight before, my heart was racing a mile per minute as I laid on the bench and positioned my hands in the desired position on the barbell. My fraternity brother counted down from three as I inhaled and exhaled repeatedly to prepare myself to lift what seemed like the weight of the world. As the countdown reached one, all at once, with the support of my spotter, I lifted the barbell, lowered it to meet my chest, and seamlessly lifted it back into place on the weight rack. Shocked and amazed, all of a sudden I gained the confidence of a giant. This was my max, and it was easy! Naturally, I gained an addiction to the high I had felt. So, every day that we were scheduled to work on our chests, this became part of our regular routine. We would start off our workout by loading the barbell with the max amount of weight we could lift, and with the support of one another, we would max out.

Then, one day, my fraternity brother told me he did not feel well, and he would not be able to join me for that week's scheduled chest day. Ambitious and full of confidence, I decided to go to the gym alone. Just like normal, I performed the regular warmups, consumed the routine dose of C4 pre-workout, and loaded the barbell with the 295 pounds. I laid on the bench, positioned my typical hand placement, inhaled, exhaled, and then after the count of three, I lifted the bar and began to lower it to my chest. And it was at that very moment that I knew I had fucked up. The only thing I could think is how I wished I had a reset button, something that would allow me to rewind time and rethink this terrible decision before actually going through with it. This time, the weight seemed unusually heavy and almost impossible to move. Fearing for my life, I slowly lowered the bar to my chest, shimmied over to the right side of the barbell, and used both hands to lift one side of the weights, freeing myself from my shameful defeat. I quickly restacked the barbell on the weight rack before anyone could see what happened, to avoid embarrassment, but I could not escape my internal uncertainty. What the hell just happened?

What happened was that I had become too dependent on my fraternity brother as my support. I got too comfortable with him always being there to help me lift the burden off of my chest, so in his absence, I did not have the strength to bear the weight on my own. Fortunately, for me, this was a reality I encountered early on, and I did not have a multi-million dollar asset depending on it. However, for many of you, this is either a reality you have had to learn the hard way, or it is inevitably coming your way, eventually, once you start to notice your market conditions change.

Digital marketing is the spotter of the leasing world. Many managers become overly dependent on the internet as their sole form of marketing. You invest 85% of your marketing dollars on Google Ads, paid ads, PPC, retargeting campaigns, etc. Then you flood your social media feeds with the occasional post about current leasing specials, and then sit back and wait for all the traffic to flow into your leasing office. Under the assumption that this is the most convenient and most affordable vertical to reach your targeted audience, you over index the majority of your funds and efforts toward digital, expecting it to bring in all the necessary traffic for a successful leasing year. To some degree, you are correct; digital marketing is imperative to your success. Maintaining a good digital footprint is 100% invaluable to your lease-up. However, much like how a spotter in the gym is there to help supplement the work you are already doing to maximize your full strength, digital marketing is also supplemental, and is used to help you meet your true branding potential, not do all the heavy lifting.

We live in the golden era of the internet. It is obnoxious how fortunate we are to live in a time where the internet is as mature as it is. There is a social media site that caters to the personalities of just about every demographic out there. You have Facebook socialites, Twitter users who are very opinionated and straight to the point, all the way to the Instagram artist and stylist. You have a platform to deploy any message, or to experiment with any advertise-ment you want, at scale! The internet has provided full empowerment to anyone who wants to take advantage of it, if you are willing to utilize its full potential. The only problem is, much like everything else in life, this golden era has an expiration date, and as the competition increases in your market, and people begin to get more tactical with their digital marketing, your competitive edge will begin to decrease.

Having a healthy balance of digital marketing and outreach marketing is essential for a successful leasing season. Depending solely on the internet to market your property is essentially crippling yourself and limiting your full potential. Many managers meet this reality but are too late to act. You invest only in digital marketing; then when your traffic slows down and you're not pulling as much engagement as you used to, you divert to the hyper-exhausted excuse that your market is overly saturated or you're just in a late market. No, what happened is your marketing strategy has no versatility, and the same stale strategy you have been using is no longer pulling response. You have plateaued, and since you have limited yourself to only social media and digital marketing, you know no other avenue of driving traffic.

The fact of the matter is that social media and digital marketing is pivotal for branding your community, but it is not everything. When it comes to really promoting your community and driving response, digital is merely supplemental marketing. You have to be willing to do the work. Earn every lead that walks through the door, by doing the work required, beyond your key board. Solely digital marketing may work for you right now, but eventually this wave will pass. Believe me, if your market has a history of leasing up year over year, chances are some developer sees it and is planning to bring new product into that market. Then, when this reality comes, and your leasing velocity slows down, and your social engagement is plummeting, it's not simply going to be because the market is over-saturated or the new supply is consuming the prospect inventory; it will be because you did not prepare yourself for the storm. You didn't allow yourself to develop the muscle that is required to endure through the hard times. That muscle is in your ability to outreach market beyond the internet. There will be a time when it is entirely up to you to push the weight of your market off your chest. There will be no internet marketing platform around that can be your spotter. The question is, are you going to have the strength to bear the weight on your own?

The Tabling Love/Hate Relationship

How you present yourself sets the standard for how the world will perceive you. As a person, the image you cast, the way you speak, and the mere expression on your face gives the people around you the opportunity to place judgement before truly even getting to know who you are. The fact is—no matter who, no matter where, no matter when, whether good or bad—the moment you walk into a room, someone in that space is placing judgement on you. This is true for you, much like it is true for your property. People prejudge your property all the time, whether that is based on your online reputation, social media presence, curb appeal, or simply how you present your property while tabling during outreach marketing. You are always on stage, being judged by potential prospects, and whether that judgement is good or bad, it is up to you to always put your best foot forward.

Tabling is one of those areas where managers often undermine the significance. When I travel to different markets, I hear things like: "Oh, we are just tabling on campus," or, "This is just the small housing fair; the big one is in the spring." You determine your tabling efforts predicated upon the significance of the event, not the value of your property.

The problem with this is that there is no such thing as a small or big first impression. Your first impression on someone is your first impression, and that is all. It is very similar to how you would present yourself at a job interview. You don't dress for the position you have; you dress for the position you want. If you are interviewing to be a basketball coach, you wouldn't walk into your interview with a tank top and gym shoes on, just because it's a coaching job. Instead, dress like you want to own the damn team. You want to look like you mean business, like you are a person of value. You may not dress in a 3-piece suit all the time, but you, for damn sure, aren't going to be wearing gym shorts. There is no such thing as being overdressed, because there is always an opportunity to impress. Similarly, when it comes to tabling, there is no such thing as over promoting your community, no matter the size of the tabling event. This is your interview with the outside world. Whether you are in an interview to be the janitor or the CEO, always make sure you bring your "A" game. The point is that you will never get a second chance at making a first impression, so always put in the effort to make it a lasting one.

Too often, I hear managers default to say, "Everyone in this market already knows who we are." Then they use this as an excuse for their lax outreach efforts. The truth is, if that were the case, your property would already be full right now, and you probably wouldn't be reading this book. I implore you to realize that your table is a further extension of your property. No matter how frequently you believe you table, and how many people you may feel you have already reached in your market, each time you table, there is a very high chance that you will be meeting someone new for the first time. Although you may know what your best effort is, and you know the value of your property, the first-time prospect that has never engaged with your community before will be formulating their opinion of you that day, for the first time, based on the experience you provide now, not the potential you have. Therefore, there is no such thing as an insignificant tabling event. Tabling should be seen as exactly that: an event, every single time. Much like any event you host, it requires proper preparation to maximize your return.

Treat every tabling event like it is a housing fair day. Honestly, you may get the same value, if not more, from marketing on an average Tuesday, than you would at the spring housing expo. The truth is that housing fairs are becoming increasingly worthless as time goes on. I agree that it's an opportune time to brand your property in front of leads, at scale. Everyone in attendance knows the type of event they are at, and in some capacity, they are looking for housing. They come in with the expectation of finding the best apartment community to commit to. Naturally, they shop around each table, looking for what the next community can offer them. They go from table to table, looking for another amenity one community can offer that the last one lacked, or another promotion to take advantage of to make them feel like they got the best deal. They get sucked into a cyclone of wanting more, more, and more, because the society we live in has conditioned us to always yearn for *more*. The issue is that when we are presented with too many options, we position ourselves to suffer from what psychologists call the *paradox of choice*.

The paradox of choice is a theory that proves, in a culture where we are overconsumed with wanting more, we are only submitting ourselves to a self-induced internal torment. Having too many options will often lead us to more discontentment and insecurity, whereas with less options, we are actually happier. For instance, if a lead had to choose between two housing communities, they would likely be more satisfied with their decision in the end. They will find more confidence that they made the right choice, because they only had to choose between the two options. Comparatively, if the same lead were forced to choose between, say, 20 different communities, they are more apt to dwell on the decision made, for months to come. They will feel uneasy with their decision. They will spend time agonizing and constantly second guessing whether or not they made the right choice.

Housing fairs are enablers of the paradox of choice. They are more cumbersome to our leads than they are helpful; not to mention that it is nearly impossible to truly distinguish your community amongst the other 20 properties without throwing the kitchen sink at every lead that crosses your path. People believe housing fairs to be the *gravy train*. They are the gold mine opportunity to get hundreds of guest cards and a shit ton of leads, without realizing that those very same leads have gone to your competition's table as well.

While property management common sense is to obsess over the housing fair and break the bank to outshine your comps, I say spend more time focusing on what everyone is not doing, opposed to what they are. What can you do that is distinctively different? Those very same tabling events that you down play to be insignificant, can actually be the more impactful, because you distinguish your property from the group. No one else is outside the most popular bar in town, tabling on a Saturday night. No one else is setting up a table at the local transit station in front of your comps community, giving away free breakfast and promotional items, as students board and depart from the bus. No one else is tabling in front of the late night dining center, at 7pm and 8pm at night. These are the things that set your community apart, because all your comps are too busy counting down the days until the next housing fair, before they get off their ass and work.

Sure, the leads you come across may not be as plentiful in volume, but they will surely prove their weight in value. Think of ways to individualize your community and your marketing efforts, instead of depending on what is *tried and true.* Do the things that others won't do that will yield massive results. Hell, I'd rather you go table in front of the on-campus dining hall on a Sunday for brunch, than spend all of your marketing dollars at housing fairs, trying to appease a bunch of students looking to mooch on everything free they can get their hands on.

Tabling is not just something you do to mark off your marketing checklist and present to the stakeholders so they feel like you're doing shit. Tabling is an event much like any other event you throw at your community. It takes proper planning, scheduling, and most importantly, execution. There is no such thing as an insignificant tabling day. It doesn't matter how small of a housing fair, or how big the campus life event. Every day is the best day to make a lasting impression on someone. Just make sure you cast your best impression, because it very well may be your last.

Self-Made Paradox

There is an old saying: "We are all self-made, but only the successful are willing to admit it." Such self-made successes glorify their position, and believe they attained their current level of success because of personal decisions made and independent actions taken to get there. They will tell you that they did things all in their own way and didn't need handouts from others. Conversely, the choice to not make a decision is a decision in itself. The choice to live stagnant in inaction is, in fact, an action on its own. Thus, this makes all of the so-called *unsuccessful* responsible for their current position as well, coining them equally *self-made.*

This is the culture many of us live by. However, somewhere along the way, the *unsuccessful* lost themselves trying to be self-made, and the self-acclaimed, self-made have become self-obsessed and narcissistic. The self-made have become pretentious narcissists that have completely neglected many of the most profound events in the processes that have contributed to their success in the first place— those who invested in their so-called success along the way. Our day-to-day decisions may be self-made, but our overall outcome comes in the absence of self all together. In any given success story, there is always someone who has contributed in one way or another to the hero's success. If you can show me a person who is entirely *self-made*, I'll show you someone who is full of shit. The truth is, no one successful is 100% self-made. Similarly, no property can sustain 100% occupancy successfully, year over year, without the contribution of other influencers in your market.

Your perspective is your driving force for everything that you do. The way you perceive what you do will dictate the way you do the things you do. Unfortunately, many managers take on the perspective of the self-made, and try to bear the weight of leasing-up their property alone. Monday through Sunday, your day begins and ends in your leasing office, making follow-up and trying to figure out how you can get leads to your community. How can you get people to buy into your brand, so much so that they are not only willing to make a 12-month commitment themselves, but also go the extra step and refer their friend to do the same? It's simple: The moment you stop thinking about your community, and start thinking about your audience, your audience will inherently start thinking about you.

In my training, I often ask my team: What are the top 5 things that consume your target audience's daily life? As a college student, what are you most interested in? I often get answers like:

- Education
- Work
- Social life
- Health and wellness
- Networking

I then proceed to ask: What are three subdivisions of each of those interests? They would often say something like:

Education – college degree, resume building, job assurance after college

Work – money to survive, work experience, broke college student

Social life – partying, hanging out with friends, fraternity/sorority

Health and wellness – staying in shape, looking their best, having food to eat

Networking – making lasting relationships, connections in desired career path, building resources

We then continue this exercise by discussing the importance of each one of these interests to our audience. Then I simply pose the question: Now that we know what is important to the student, and what consumes their interest at its core—where does your community come in? On this laundry list of things that consume the average college student's mind on a daily basis, when do they have time to think about your property?

Dr. Martin Luther King said, "Life's most persistent and urgent question is, 'what are you doing for others?'" What value can you create that will make you a priority in your audience's eye? Service is the true elevation of your community. What can you offer outside of the walls of your leasing office that your audience can benefit from? Your audience will never think of you as a priority until you can position your community as a place of value.

The easiest way to offer further value in your community is to be able to remove yourself from the confinement of your leasing office, and infuse your community into the things that your audience is constantly thinking about on a daily basis. How can your community influence the college student's education, work, social life, health, and networking? How can you bring value in the way your lead needs it? The answer is what Andrew Davis, *Author and keynote speaker*, eloquently describes as *brandscaping*.

Brandscaping is the ability to abandon the self-made ideology and realize that *"a rising tide lifts all ships."* Self-

made is a perspective designed for sure failure in the property management world. It's a losing formula. Figure out who your target audience is, what they are interested in, and what drives them. Then, if it is something you can't physically offer, figure out who can, and partner with them. Davis says, *"Figure out who has your next customer as their current customer."* Once you figure out who has a product that your potential prospects buy, figure out how to partner with them. Figure out what value you can offer to another company that can greatly benefit their business, and can lead to you marketing your brand in a place highly populated with your target audience. Give value to that business, so your relationship will be lasting and mutually beneficial.

Former President Barack Obama said, *"...when we succeed, we succeed because of our individual initiative, but also because we do things together."* Instead of maintaining the self-made mentality, adopt humility; humility in that recognizing that you cannot accomplish everything on your own does not mean you are inadequate; rather, it is quite the opposite. Anyone who has reached success in anything did not get there alone. Humble your way to success, because *self-made* is a loser's mentality. Success is found in the absence of self. It is measured by your willingness to abundantly service others, and as long as you make sure that someone else is okay, the market will always make sure that you are okay.

CHAPTER 4

Bag the First Date

Hitch Leasing Principle on Effective Follow-Ups

"Daydreams are for private time. When you're in the room, be in the room; concentrate... focus... People respond when you respond to them."

There is a common fallacy that has plagued the property management world, infecting everyone in its path. It's the idiom that "you are only as good as your ability to follow up," the belief that as long as you consistently reach out to your leads, the more probable they are to sign a lease with you. So, by following this recipe, the first thing managers do is instruct their leasing agents to sit down, call every lead on the dashboard until they're blue in the face, and make sure no leaf is left unturned—because, as long as you maintain consistent contact with your leads, you are bound to close on them. Right?

The problem with this formula is that when you solely focus on the quantity of the follow-ups made, you neglect the purpose of why you are making the calls in the first place: the people. It is almost as if you get too invested in the outcome of simply signing the next lease, and you try to bypass the most important part of the process: actually caring about the person on the other end of the phone. Inky Johnson said, *"Be careful when you're reaching for the stars that the people around you don't get burned up from the heat."* In other words, don't over-consume yourself with the outcome so much that you do so at the expense of those around, or in this case, your leads and their well-being. It is almost to the point that people are so ambitious that they are blinded by their own ambition and don't recognize the collateral damage.

Have you ever reviewed your leasing activity reports, to police your prospects, and noticed that your team has sent out an overwhelming amount of copy and paste emails to leads, instead of actually making calls? Have you ever stopped to question why this may be? Your leasing agents should know better than that. You spend countless hours training them; how can they be so neglectful? I would argue that it's not necessary neglect on your leasing agent's behalf of what needs to be done, but more so in the midst of the storm they simply lack the bandwidth to effectively execute on all demands. Through all the tasks thrown their way in a day, they lose sight of why follow-ups need to be done in the first place, let alone paying much attention to the quality of those they make. For instance, as managers, you task your leasing agents with calling the entire lead dashboard, calling all residents with the intent to renew, and calling all guarantors to see if you can expedite the leasing process. Essentially, you have tasked your leasing agent with over 100 follow-ups to make, and have the expectation that they complete them before the end of their 4-hour shift; not to mention that they still must go out and market, post on social media, log in all the packages, collect rent payments, handle incoming customers, and the list goes on. Naturally, with so many things on their plate, their intent quickly shifts from the quality of the follow-up made, and how well it is executed, to the quantity of the follow-ups they make, and how many they can get done in one shift, simply for job security.

Making effective follow-ups is not about the quantity of attempts made, but rather how you can quantify EACH attempt you make. As the manager, you should never task your team with the expectation to call every single lead in your pipeline, all in one shift. That will surely dilute the quality of the call. Instead, assign a controlled amount of follow-ups for each consultant to focus on daily. This way, your consultant will not obsessively try to complete all of their follow-ups solely to check it off their task list, and can actually focus on what is being communicated. Having each leasing consultant make 15 effective follow-ups that will eventually lead a prospect further down the leasing funnel, outweighs making 100 hallow follow-ups, simply transferring data any day.

The point is that follow-up calls only work if they are properly executed. Proper execution takes time, attention to detail, intent, care, and most of all, focus. This level of focus required to execute a proper follow-up is what inspired our fourth Hitch Leasing Principle: *"Daydreams are for private time. When you're in the room, be in the room; concentrate... focus... People respond when you respond to them."* Follow-ups are about being attentive, caring, and focusing on the person themselves, not solely the outcome of the call.

There is no better way to display a proper follow-up call than to dissect what our dating coach, Hitch, does after meeting Sara Melas for the first time, and reaching out to her, hoping to score a first date. Knowing that he did not secure her contact information in the most conventional way, he took an unorthodox, very original approach. Unearthing the fact that Melas ran the gossip column, in the *Standard Newspaper*, from their previous conversation, Hitch decided to send Melas a special delivery to her office. The package contained a walkie-talkie that prompted the following conversation:

Hitch: I hate it when a guy calls a girl who did not give him her number. So this is me not calling. Over.

Sara: Yes, you're right. This is much less invasive.

Hitch: I've been thinking about that sign on your forehead. And I was wondering if you'd mind taking it down for dinner Friday night. Over.

Sara: I can't. I have a couple of parties I have to hit.

Hitch: Yeah… gossip never sleeps.

Sara: Not till about 4 a.m.

Hitch: Saturday?

Sara: I have a date.

Hitch: Do you know the definition of "perseverance," Miss Melas?

Sara: An excuse to be obnoxious?

Hitch: Continuing in a course of action... without regard to discouragement, opposition, or previous failure. Over.

Sara: Okay, Webster, how do I get rid of you?

Hitch: Breakfast, Sunday. And you can barely even call that a date. You do that with out-of-town relatives that you don't even like. Over.

Sara: Okay, I guess I could do Sunday.

Hitch: You forgot to say "over." Over.

Sara: This conversation's over as soon as you tell me when and where.

Hitch: 7 a.m., North Cove Marina. Over and out.

Beyond his staggering charisma and unprecedented originality, look at the execution of this follow-up call. First off, he recognized that his approach may be a little invasive, so he acknowledged it right away to break the ice. He then revisited a monumental moment from their previous encounter, by asking Miss Melas to take the sign off her forehead and join him for a date. This allowed Miss Melas to relive the high she experienced upon their last encounter, which made way for this conversation to further resonate with her. He persisted to his objective of setting the first date, despite all objections she threw his way, and he was focused. Not necessarily focused on sealing the deal, he was attentive and responsive to what Miss Melas was saying, and responded accordingly. He did not pick up the phone and just regurgitate information about how great dating him would be, and all the great amenities the Cove Marina had to offer. He simply focused on booking the date. These are all qualities of an effective follow-up call.

Now think, a call like this in student housing, on average, can take about 3–5 minutes, give or take. That's not factoring in the recon your agent must do before making the call, and the activity they must record after the call. This overall process can average about 6–8 minutes a call, if done correctly, and often times even more if a lead has questions that we have yet to provide answers to. Similarly, if the lead does not answer the phone, you leave a voice mail, followed by an email, discussing your attempt to call. The process takes time to effectively make a follow-up. Now, imagine paying this much attention to detail and building this level of rapport with your leads or prospective renewals when you have 100 calls to make. It's impossible! Physically, there just is not enough time in a day.

It's not that we are only as good as our ability to follow up, because everyone has the *ability* to make a phone call or send an email. If not, you should be having another, less pleasant conversation with your staff. It's more in line with what the late Zig Ziglar, *American author, salesman, and motivational speaker*, said long ago, "It is your attitude, more than your aptitude, that will determine your altitude." If you change the way you think about making follow-ups, and the way you perceive why you make follow- ups, you will change the way that you execute your follow-ups. Encourage effective follow-ups as the standard in your office, opposed to something you do just to mark off your task list. Of course, it is important to make sure no lead goes unattended. We always want to make sure we are keeping up with each lead in a timely fashion. However, an effective follow-up call tomorrow is better than a task list follow-up today. Change your mind from focusing on the number of follow-ups made, and concentrate more on the effort, focus, and care behind each follow-up you make, and I guarantee you will see a vast difference in the amount of leases you close. But it all starts with focus.

A System Is a Lifestyle, Not a Practice

One of the more simple, yet profound analogies I had been told very early in my property management career, was articulated to me by my area manager at the time. Just a few months into my position as a leasing manager, I met him during one of his site visits to my property. After he finished his inspection, he sat with me to debrief. He asked me where I felt my greatest room for improvement was. What was it that I struggled with most, and where could I use support? At the time, the list was more than I can count on my hands. Hell, I wanted to tell him it would be easier to list the few things that I actually understood, opposed to the endless list of what I didn't. However, in an effort to save face, and my job, I defaulted to what seemed to be my number one fault: time management.

Managing my personal time wasn't necessarily the hard part, although that could use help too. It was more so juggling the responsibility of managing my schedule on top of all of my leasing agent's schedule, and making sure we were making the most effective use of our day. "Where the hell am I supposed to find the time to make sure all of my leasing agents are all doing what they are supposed to be doing, and still manage to accomplish everything I am responsible for before the day is over?

Seeming to avoid my questions, he began to explain the difference between two common childhood toys: the standard Hot Wheels car, and the more advanced, wind-up toy car. Hot Wheels require your undivided attention. With much force, you can push a Hot Wheels car in the direction you want it to go, but eventually it inevitably comes to a stop. It is going to require constant micro-management and redirection in order to assure it gets to the desired destination. However, the wind-up car, with the right motivation at the beginning, is more self-sufficient. Once you wind it up, provide the right amount of momentum, and point it in the right direction, you can put it on the ground and let it take its course. He further explained that when you micro-manage other people's work, very seldom does that leave enough time for you to focus on your own. The type of leader you want to be is one who can get your team wound up within the first 5 minutes of their shift, start them in the right direction toward the common goal, take your eyes off them, and be confident that they will reach the destination on their own. Thus, it will minimize your wasted energy by micro-managing, and afford you the time to dedicate toward other responsibilities. In other words, in order to be effective at managing my time, I had to develop a system.

Systems, at the very foundation of the concept, are designed to maximize your time. However, in the absence of such a system, you will often times find yourself trying to manage the empty gaps in your staffing schedule by delegating monotonous, tedious tasks, just to get your staff through their scheduled shift. William Penn, *American writer*, once said, "Time is what we want most but what we use worst." The most valuable investment you can make is your time. The way you spend your time is more important than how you spend your money, because you can always make more money but you can never get more time. Time is like currency, and how you spend it is going to dictate your ROI. Unfortunately, many managers are unconscious, habitual time killers, and daily subject themselves to watching their investment crash.

Too often, managers in student housing approach each day with a *fly by the seat of your pants* mentality, where they decide their team's course of action as the days go along, based on mere impulse instead of a premeditated strategy. Sure, you will create a huge marketing calendar for the upcoming month, but on a day-to-day basis, you wait until your staff come into the office, one by one, look at you with their puppy dog eyes, and beg you for some direction. Then you instruct them to do their routine daily task, followed by calling all the leads in your dashboard. Next thing you know, they are stuck behind the reception desk, organizing resident packages, anticipating the moment for a customer to walk through the door, bleeding the clock of every last second it has left, until finally, their shift ends and they can go home.

Follow-up calls are essential, but they only work if you have a system. John Maxwell said, *"Motivation will get you going, but habits will get you there."* Systems are your daily habits that you instill within your office that, with repetition, will automate your leasing process to success. When it comes to your follow-up system, you want to compartmentalize your prospect pool. Identify who your hot leads, warm leads, and cold leads are. Then, once you know your lead's status, create a metric for how often each lead needs to be followed up with. For instance, hot leads will be contacted every 24 hours, as they are right on the fence, and with the right motivation are more susceptible to sign while the idea is at the top of their mind. Warm leads will be contacted every 48 hours; although they are still interested in your property, they may need a little more convincing before they are ready to commit. Lastly, cold leads, who probably just expressed interest to get your free shit, of course may not be interested in signing a lease right now, but they still should be contacted every 72 hours to further lead them through the leasing funnel.

Now, with a system in line, instead of telling your team to call the dashboard, you can be more strategic with how you are utilizing your team and maximizing your time. You know who your hot leads are, that if you call today, you can close; and you also know your warm leads that may need just a little more TLC. Now you are not aimlessly having your team call every lead in your pipeline simply because they are 72 hours out; you can follow up with more precision.

Words of wisdom from A. A. Milne (creator of Winnie the Pooh) say it best: "Organization is what you do before you do something, so that when you do it, it's not all mixed up." Organize your prospect inventory. Create a metric to help add structure to how frequent you should follow up with each lead. Then, when instructing your team to execute, you can be more meticulous. Inefficiency is a sure path to ineffectiveness. Create an effective follow-up structure for your team now, so when the time comes, all you have to do is wind them up, point them in the right direction, and let your system take the wheel.

Develop a Follow-Up Strategy

The most common mistake leasing consultants make when it comes to making their follow-ups is that they do so at their own convenience. Think about the average work day. If you open your office at 9am, assuming your opening staff come in on time and complete all opening duties thoroughly, your office will be in perfect shape around 9:45am, give or take 15 minutes. Then, after your morning team meeting, where you discuss the direction for the day, it won't be until at least 10am before your leasing agent would actually start their day. Finally, after gaining their bearings theoretically, they sit down and begin making follow-ups. One phone call after another, one voicemail after another, until finally, you get the occasional pick up from the student that whispers in the strikingly faint voice, "Can I call you back after my class?" Then, click... hangs up. Meanwhile, you sit back, waiting patiently, hoping that they actually stay true to their word.

It won't be for another 72 hours before you reach out

to those same leads—chances are, using the same failed technique as before, but hoping for a different outcome. This, by definition, is called insanity: doing the same thing over and over again but expecting a different result. The question is, why? Often times, I find this a calculated decision by leasing consultants—intentionally making follow-ups midmorning, under the assumption that any earlier is too early to call anyone. So they wait until after 10am to make follow-up calls, hoping to catch their leads at a reasonable hour, only to meet the same fate—the ever consistent voicemail.

The problem here is not that the timing is inconvenient for your leads, but more so because you are picking times that are more convenient for you. Too often, people justify this phenomenon with statements like: "If it were me, I wouldn't answer the phone that early in the morning." The issue is that you are spending too much time thinking about yourself, and not enough time thinking about the lead. Midmorning calls are ideal for you because you have had the time to complete all your morning duties, set up your day, and can finally get around to making your calls. However, think about your target audience for a moment. There is no other industry in sales, besides student housing, where all of your target audience is all in one place, all at one time. Think about it; at just about any university in the country, with respects to the few that deviate from this rule, from around 8am–2pm, you will find about 85% of the student body on campus. So now your midmorning call that was intended on being more convenient, now serves as more of an inconvenience for your leads, because you're constantly calling them during their class, which then leads to them forwarding you to their voicemail or a first class ticket to the block list.

Now, many would argue that as long as you leave a compelling enough voicemail, and stress enough urgency, your lead will most certainly give you a call back. The truth is, voicemail is a dying technology. Checking a voicemail nowadays has become more of a chore than a convenience. It is inefficient, and creates another obligation for our leads to add to their to-do list. Think of the last time you saw a voicemail notification and got excited about it. "Oh, my god, I'm so happy I got your voicemail," said no one ever. In fact, I would venture to assume that you are more apt to simply clear that nasty notification from your screen, until you find a more convenient time to check it at a later date, than you are to answer it right away. The fact is that just as much as your leasing agents hate leaving a lead a voicemail, your lead shares the same level of enthusiasm for receiving them.

Now, I'm not saying mornings are the most ideal time to make all your follow-up calls; in fact, unless you're up at the crack of dawn calling, mornings are arguably the most ineffective. Nor am I saying to stop using any form of asynchronous communication. All I am saying is that in order to maximize your follow-up efforts, you must develop a strategy. In order to develop a strategy, you must think less of what is convenient for you, and think more about what is suitable for your leads.

If you are aware that your target audience is the college student demographic, start thinking like a college student. What is the first thing a student does when they wake up in the morning? They reach for their cell phone, sift through social media, review missed text messages, etc. Knowing this, use it to your advantage. If you haven't had luck calling this lead during peak leasing hours, schedule a text message to meet that student in the morning. This way, if you feel a phone call in the morning is too invasive, your text message will serve the same purpose. If you're constantly leaving voice messages in the middle of the work day, that is because your lead is probably in class. Be strategic with your calls, and reach out to your leads when they are out of class, and it is more probable that they will answer their phones. If you have not been able to reach a guarantor of a lease, it's probably because they work the same hours in a day that you do. When you're busy, chances are so are they. If this is the case, think about when it is most ideal to reach you, or when are you most likely to check your emails. Know your target audience, and familiarize yourself with the typical schedule. When are the peak lunch hours, breaks for passing period, etc.? That way, instead of burdening your team with making follow-up calls during the day, they can spend that same time and energy doing more effective tasks that will drive leasing. Timing is everything, so use it to your advantage when scheduling your follow-up calls.

There are many strategies out there that can greatly increase your follow-up reach, but they all have one thing in common: The follow-up cannot be on your terms; it has to be on the consumer's. The moment that you stop thinking about making follow-ups when it is most convenient for you, and start thinking about what is most efficient for your leads, you will begin to maximize the amount of actual contacts you make, opposed to the overwhelming slant of failed attempts that result in voicemail. Develop a strategy for your follow-up calls so you can finally allow the concept of the voicemail to rest in peace.

Is Mass Marketing Effective?

Questioning the effectiveness of using mass communication as a form of follow-up is the modern day leasing equivalent to the philosophical debate: If a tree falls in the forest, and no one is around to hear it, does it make a sound? Many argue the logical affirmative that sound is not contingent upon human witness; therefore, it does not require an audience for validation. The opposing perspective would agree with George Orwell's (*English novelist, 1984*) theory that *"nothing exists except through human consciousness."* In other words, there is no reality without human experience. Therefore, the tree does not make a sound, because no one was there to witness it. Now, I don't mean to fall too deep into a quantum mechanics rabbit hole, but it does pose a very interesting question about sending mass email blasts or blanket text messages as a form of follow-up. If the intended recipient never reads the memo, can you really call it a message? And if the message is never received, is it in fact a follow-up?

I remember the grand opening of my first new development deal, in Allendale, MI. My team and I were charged with excitement for this event. We had tons of games and giveaways that students would be crazy to refuse. We were planning to transport students to and from campus in a decked out party bus. We had vendor sponsorship from Buffalo Wild Wings, Chick-fil-A, Red Bull, and more! This event was going to be of the chain! For the weeks leading up to the event, we marketed like mad men. You would've thought it was the Cirque Du Soleil coming to town. It seemed like everyone in the market knew about this event! So, the week of, following our predetermined marketing plan, we sent out a mass email to all of our leads, on Monday, marketing the grand opening. We then followed the email by sending two mass text messages to our prospects that week, one on that Tuesday, and another on Thursday, the day of the big event. To our surprise, annoyed by our persistent marketing, one of our leads, by the name of Jacob, replied in big bold letters: "FUCK OFF!" My senior community assistant, having a personal relationship with the lead, replied, "Sad to hear you won't be able to make it, Jacob!" Jacob replied, "OMG! I'm so sorry; I didn't know it was an actual person sending out these messages. Yes, I will be there!"

It's hard to pass judgement on Jacob for the way he

responded, because his reaction represents 90% of the people reading this right now. Sure, his methods were a little aggressive but, mentally, he is in line with the mindset of the majority of people today. Think about the last time you received a blanket text and read it from start to finish. When was the last time you saw that 5-digit phone number come across your notifications, got excited to read it, and actually paid attention to the content? More accurately, I would venture to say you are probably guilty of opening a similar message, seeing that it is Verizon or some other retailer trying to sell another iPhone, and matching iPad at 50% off. Chances are, you probably deleted it before reading to the end, just so you could clear it from your message feed, forgetting it ever happened.

William James, *American philosopher and psychologist*, once said, *"The deepest principle in human nature is our craving to be appreciated."* In other words, it is a basic human need to feel some level of significance. We crave to feel important. People don't like being seen as just another spoke in a wheel, or just another spam recipient on the other side of an advertisement text. So, Jacob's reaction, although ill-mannered, may represent a similar feeling that a large percent of your leads are feeling. Sending mass marketing mediums, like template emails and blanket text messages, defy the very concept of making our leads feel significant.

Now, I don't want my words to be misconstrued. I don't believe mass communication is bad. I am saying that it is very hard to measure its effectiveness, because it's virtually impossible to know who is really consuming the content, and who is simply clicking through it just to clear their feed. We can send out the message, and hope that people are seeing it, but there is no way to know for sure how they interpret your content. I have personally seen success with email marketing and mass text messages, but we cannot solely depend on these mediums to drive our leasing. Unfortunately, many managers do just that. You become satisfied with sending a mass email out once a week, and you expect it to drive leasing. The truth is, even when done correctly, on average, you're probably only going to receive a click through rate of about 15%–20% on a good email.

Asynchronous communication has and always will be a huge asset in property management space, especially when it comes to leasing. My concern is that with many managers, your efforts stop with mass communication. I would encourage you to continue to send out your message as a supplemental marketing medium, but take it a step further. Utilizing the maturity of mobile technology and the social media space to personalize your follow-ups can make all the difference. There are mobile apps available, like Google Voice, that issue you a standard, 10-digit number, specific to the area code of your choice, which will give you the same functionality of a typical mobile phone. You have access to text messaging, phone calling, and masking, where you can use your personal mobile phone but operate as if you're using the assigned Google phone number. This way, you can reach out to those same leads, personalize your text, and allow your lead to feel that significance they are craving from your text message. Your lead will be more inclined to answer the message because it is a standard phone number, oppose to the 5-digit alternatives.

Similarly, just about every social media platform nowadays has a direct message option available that you can utilize to reach out to hard-to-reach leads. I know, it seems a little invasive and impersonal. I would argue, so did online dating, 10 years ago. If I had a dollar for every time I heard someone say that online dating was weird, or passed judgement at the mere thought of it, I would be swimming in money! Now look at it—everyone swiping right on Tinder, and fishing the Plenty of Fish for love. The fact is, our social norms have changed, and the era of social media has revolutionized the way we communicate with one another. People are more susceptible to communicating online, as that is where they dedicate an ample amount of their time anyway. Utilize this function to contact those hard-to-reach leads; in fact, make it more convenient for them. The great thing about all direct messaging functions is that each one of them has the *read receipt* function, which will tell you whether or not your lead has actually seen the message, or if they are simply ignoring you. Either way, it allows you to gauge their interest level.

Living in an era where we have met at full maturity of the internet, our ability to communicate with one another is at scale. We no longer are confined by the limitations of mass email being the x factor of our follow-up strategy, or dealing with the uncertainty of whether or not our leads are getting the message. Sure, we will never really be able to determine whether or not our leads are actually reading the content we put out. Maybe we will always have to agree to disagree with whether or not the falling tree in a forest in fact makes a sound. But thanks to the advancement of the social world and the mobile revolution, you won't have to be concerned either way, because you now have the tools to knock down the whole forest. Your leads are bound to hear that!

CHAPTER 5

Sweep Them Off Their Feet

Hitch Leasing Principle on The Tour

"Life is not about the amount of breaths you take; it's about the moments that take your breath away."

This is it. You're in the high stakes medal round now—the moment where 8 out of 10 leads believe they will figure out all they need to know about a community before making a commitment. This is your first date. Interestingly, this is the moment dating and leasing draw a distinctive difference. In dating, you will rarely see someone ready to commit after just one date. In fact, if you did see this, you might question that person and even suggest that they are moving too fast. Hitch would suggest that he needs three dates to get you to this point—the point where both parties are certain they can see further commitment with one another. However, in the leasing, more often than not, this is it. You get one tour, one pitch, and one opportunity to sweep your lead off their feet. This is where you distinguish your community from the other 30 options in the market. Your tour, your first date, and your lead's first impression all happens right now! This is where the magic happens, and where better to learn magic from than the most magical place on earth—Disneyland.

Think about the maturity of a 5-year-old's imagination. As a child, you can undoubtedly believe that magic exists! At the sight of a carpet, if you sit down in the right place, pull the edge back just enough, and sing, "A Whole New World," you can venture on a magic carpet ride. Or maybe, at the sight of a lamp, with the right conviction, and if you rub it just enough, a genie will appear and grant you three wishes. Think about your five-year-old niece that truly believes Elsa is actually capable of building an ice castle out of thin air. As a child, virtually anything is possible. There is no limit to how far our mind can stretch. However, as adults, we grow up and start to get more of a grasp on what is *real* and what is not, slowly laying to rest our inner child, and sentencing our once vibrant imagination to an insidious death.

However, in the world where dreams come true, no matter how old you are, your imagination is free to run wild. Disneyland has mastered the art of creating an experience for everyone who steps foot in their park, from the winter wonderland, snowflakes illuminating the night sky, to all of your favorite childhood personalities, in full character. The way the park smells, to the unique taste of their pickles, every small detail has been tailored around the customer experience. Even looking at the most granular level of detail, when you walk into retail stores at the park, you will notice that all the items for sale are color coded and organized accordingly. Walt Disney focused on the smallest of details to assure that each and every customer that attends his parks has a meaningful experience.

Although your leads may not outright express it at first, they are looking for the apartment rendition of the Disneyland experience. They want to be swept off their feet. However, all too often, managers get comfortable, and they begin to forget about the key fundamentals that can have a massive impact on a lead's first impression—the small things that make a huge impact. This is an example of one falling victim to the *law of familiarity*. Oftentimes, I witness managers who have been at their property for long periods of time; and they get comfortable and complacent, where they otherwise would not: staff members eating lunch at the front desk; outdated event flyers posted around the community, if they are posted at all; forgetting to assure the model unit is properly opened; and the list goes on. Just because this is your 9–5, 5 days a week, you become insensitive to things that mattered before. Unfortunately, those little things that you are now neglecting may be the first things your lead notices, with a fresh set of eyes, experiencing your community for the first time.

As property managers, when considering new traffic

visiting your community, one of the most urgent and persistent questions you should be asking is, "How can I leave a lasting impression?" This frame of mind is what inspired our fifth Hitch Leasing Principle for sweeping your leads off their feet on a tour: "Life is not about the amount of breaths you take; it's about the moments that take your breath away." Focus on the small details that will wildly impress your leads. From the refreshing scent that welcomes them as soon as they enter your leasing office, to the enthusiastic leasing agents that greet them upon entry, every detail should set the standard for the experience you plan to cast. Assure that all the free weights in the 24-hour gym are uniform and in chronological order. When they walk into your model, make your leads feel at home with the smell of freshly baked cookies in the oven, to compliment a flawless show unit, painting the picture of what their home could look like if they lived there. Think of the last time you went on vacation and stayed at a resort. Emulate the experience you had, and create that for your leads. This entire first experience should feel like the roller coaster ride of a lifetime for your leads.

Age does not require the absence of imagination. Most often, we begin to question the existence of all of our childhood fantasies because, somewhere along the path of life, we have been let down. Someone told us Santa Clause didn't exist, or maybe you caught Dad sneaking to your pillow, instead of the tooth fairy. Something in life has forced us to think that such wonders could never actually exist in the world that we know. Your prospective leads may be suffering the same fate: scarred by past rental experiences, never believing the perfect community is out there, so they just have to settle for the better of all evils. It is up to you to bring out their inner child, show them that magic does exist, and allow them to imagine the endless possibilities of what it would be like to live in your community. Take your leads on that magic carpet ride, taking their breath away at every amenity provided, and just like that, they will experience a whole new world.

Intimacy Is Everything

We don't just walk into a restaurant for the hell of it, without being hungry, much like we don't voluntarily go to the eye doctor because it's a walk in the park. Similarly, people don't just walk into your community because it seems like a cool thing to do. When a lead enters your community and inquires about a tour, it is often because they are experiencing some form of discontentment elsewhere. Maybe they are dissatisfied with their current community because maintenance teams respond to work orders at the pace of molasses, and they are tired of having to go to the public bathroom to take a shit because their toilet is still broke. Maybe the apartment community they currently live in is significantly jumping rates but not offering anything new in return, so they are looking to find value elsewhere. Whatever the case may be, there is a reason why that lead is sitting in your office. But how will you ever know without taking the time to figure it out?

This is where many leasing agents fail. You are too vested in the short-term success of signing a lease, and you lose sight of the long-term objective of providing your lead with a place they will truly love to call home. As a leasing agent, with such demand to meet leasing goals, it's natural to see this as opportunity to write your own pay check, looking at prospects as if they are walking dollar signs and, consequently, unknowingly treating them accordingly. Think about it; when was the last time you looked at a $100 bill and asked Franklin what he wanted to be spent on? Never! Instead, you took that money and cashed out on dinner for two, or bought a new pair of fancy shoes without blinking an eye. If this is how you look at your leads—as just another commission check or another number to get you closer to your monthly lease goal—then I can guarantee that you will continue to approach your tours with the same focus: "What can they do for me?"

The problem is that you are acting out of selfish intent. You are constantly thinking about the sale, without first romancing your lead. If this were a first date, you are thinking about hooking up instead of how you can build a meaningful relationship. This is a recipe for failure. As a result, you rush your tour, talk about nothing but the property the entire time, and never get to know who is on the other side of the table, or why they are there in the first place—unfortunately, neglecting the fact that most don't buy products; they buy people.

Instead, realize that 100% of your leads are people, 100% of your guarantors are people, and likewise, 100% of your leasing agents are people. And no matter how hard the person may be to read, there are very basic essential needs that drive all human decisions, the most relevant here being the need for connection. As humans, our very existence depends on our ability to build interpersonal connections, affinity, and love with one another. So, oftentimes, when your lead comes to your community, they are itching to fulfill this craving; they just don't know it yet. This is why it is so important for your leasing agents to invest in building rapport.

Building rapport is the single, most important thing you can do on any tour! This process can last anywhere from 5 minutes (which, if it does, you should be concerned) to 35 minutes, and sometimes even longer. But no matter how long this takes, it needs to happen. This is where you establish intimacy with your lead, create a common ground, establish a connection and, essentially, earn their trust. And once you earn a person's trust, it is amazing the amount of influence you can have over the decisions they make — in this case, where they choose to live.

Although building rapport is the most important aspect of any tour, it is also the most undervalued. Too often, leasing professionals misconstrue rapport building with small talk, simply asking meaningless questions just to buffer the awkward, intermittent time between walking from the leasing office to the show unit: "So, how was the drive over? Crazy weather we're having, right? Did you watch the game last night?" These questions literally mean nothing! They are irrelevant! This form of small talk is simply the transferal of data—information that goes in one ear and out the other.

The trick to stimulating meaningful conversations is asking meaningful questions. Ask questions with the intent to get to know your lead deeper than what is on the surface. How? Merely use words, like *most* or *happiest*, to rouse conversation. Using charging words like this requires your lead to physiologically survey through all of their experiences, and regurgitate what is the most significant to them. Let's face it; we are all a little narcissistic by nature, so when you give someone the opportunity to talk about themselves, they are going to run with it if you ask the right questions: "If you had to choose, what are the **most** important things to you in your next home?" Or… "When you think of your dream home, what is it about it that makes you **happiest**?"

Just like that, you have opened the flood gates. Your lead is going to let it all go. In this moment, your lead is going to give you the study guide to your upcoming exam. Now, all you have to do is listen! Don't daydream about how much money this is going to add to your commission check. Pay attention! That way, when it's your turn to speak, you will have something meaningful to say, and you'll have all the information you need to ace this test.

The truth is, there are a lot of very intelligent people behind the creation of your apartment community. From the overall concept, design, architecture, etc., people have endowed ample time in manufacturing what is now the finished product you all occupy today. So, if you really wanted to sit down with the lead and tell them everything there is to know about your property, you could probably talk to them for a week straight. However, the fact is that your lead doesn't give a shit. The only reason why they are in your office is because they are looking for justification for considering this place in the first place. They want to see if they can even picture themselves living in your community.   By you simply listing off amenity after amenity as you breeze through the property tour, ask yourself what the difference is between the information you are saying, and the information given on your website? What distinguishes you, listing off amenities, from the brochure they have in their hand, which also lists off amenities? Without rapport—absolutely nothing. They can get all of the information you are providing, online, from the comfort of their couch.

Divorce the practice of being a walking brochure and simply listing amenity after amenity on your tours. Instead, take the time to sit down with your lead and get to know them. Figure out what makes them tick. Identify common ground, and genuinely develop a connection with one another. Then use all the information you gather to paint your lead a picture of why your community is the new home they've been looking for.

Knowledge Is Not Power

It was the summer of 2015, when five of my buddies and I, or what we called, our Squadron, decided we wanted to celebrate life by going on a guys' trip to Portland, Oregon. Having very limited knowledge of the city, beyond its obvious liberal, eclectic culture, we decided to fully immerse in the tourist experience—site seeing, bar hopping, the whole nine yards—and this was all before noon. I had my first burger with peanut butter on it, from Killer Burger, because… why not, right? We're in Portland. By the way, if you have never had peanut butter on a burger before, thank me later. Nonetheless, we were living our best life, until it dawned on us that the person responsible for booking our hotel had yet to secure our reservation, and it just so happened that there had been a major business convention in town that weekend, so availability was scarce.

Frantically, we all put our heads together to devise a plan. Apprehensively, and slightly influenced by the subtle buzz we had going, we decided to walk around downtown Portland to see if there were any hotels with a suite available to house our party. Meeting failure after failure, we finally found a signature suite that accommodated us, right in the heart of downtown—the perfect location for our 4-day getaway.

There was something interesting that I found along our journey from hotel to hotel, which was very simple, yet at the same time, very insightful. Naturally, after walking many miles up and down the city streets, coupled with the inherent dehydration that came as a result of the cocktails from earlier, we were parched by the time we got to the first hotel. Fortunately, each hotel we visited had its own unique selection of infused water. Overjoyed by the hospitality, before even addressing the concierge, I sprinted to the water selection to see what was on the menu. The first cup was a very refreshing cucumber and mint number. The next hotel had a really nice mandarin citrus infusion. And this pattern continued. It seemed as if every hotel had their own patented water, and I wanted to try them all! So we made a game of it, and went from hotel to hotel to see which water was the best. This game lasted upward to about an hour, until we finally found the anomaly hotel. The accommodation we actually decided to stay in was the game changer! Not only did they offer all of the water selections as the others did previously, they also had a watermelon mint infusion that took my taste buds for a whirl! I found my water of choice, and I am not sure if this played a role in our decision to stay in this hotel or not, but I do know it was the icing on the cake!

Notice that the only need that I had was one of basic human necessity. I was dehydrated, and I yearned to find some water to quench my thirst. Simple tap water could have sufficed, or even a chilled, bottled water would have done just fine, but it would not have made nearly as great of an impact. There would have been nothing significant about that experience, and certainly nothing memorable enough to write about in a book. However, these hotels took a very practical need and created an experience out of it for the customer.

Now, imagine if you could take this same concept and apply it to the way that you give tours. Imagine if your leads simply fixed their mind to walk into your leasing office to satisfy a basic student necessity: the need for refuge during their college years. Imagine if you had the ability to take that small gesture and create an experience of a lifetime for your leads, so memorable that not only would they choose to live with you, but they would also go out and tell everyone in their friends group, and their parents, and even take a selfie and blast it all over social media, telling their social network about how earth shattering their experience at your community was, and how they can't wait to live there!

That is the power of rapport building; the power you gain by getting to know your leads before showing them around the community. You now have the ability to infuse your tour with the perfect flavor to satisfy their palette precisely. Unfortunately, many leasing agents completely squander this opportunity, and if they do it at all, build rapport simply for formality, never utilizing the information gained to shape the lead's experience. Too often, you get stuck in a cookie cutter sales pitch, generalizing every person who goes on a tour, and assuming that everyone is excited to hear about the massive pool parties you have, not taking into account that this particular lead may be a biology student that would rather spend their time studying in an individual study lounge, opposed to raging out poolside. You assume that everyone enjoys binge drinking endless amounts of coffee, but what if your lead doesn't like coffee at all? You know what they say: When you assume, you only make an ASS out of U and ME—in this case, you and your lead.

Somewhere down the line, we have been brainwashed with the idiom that knowledge is power. This proves that it is not knowledge alone that is power, but applied knowledge that truly gives you the upper hand. Always think about how you can utilize the information you gain from building rapport, to further create value for your leads. Stop thinking about the property, and start thinking about the people. If your prospect vocalized that they are a very outdoorsy person, then emphasize the fact that you have a beautiful hammock garden that provides the perfect platform to embrace the array of colors that dress the autumn trees, or is a perfect place to relax under quiet summer nights, with not a cloud in the sky. If your lead tells you they are really into fitness, make the 24-hour fitness center a huge deal, and even talk about how you occasionally host fun events, like puppy yoga, in your yoga center, to make working out fun for everyone.

Take it a step further, and really figure out what is driving your lead. Oftentimes, we approach our next purchase by calculating what we want, not necessarily what we need. Dive a little deeper, and unearth your lead's *why*. What is definitively different about your community, and why does your lead need this? Are they in the Vet Med program, have late classes, and as a result have limited transportation because public transit stops running early? Walking home as a young lady at 10pm can be dangerous. Luckily, your community is .2 miles away from the Vet Med Hall, and is a quick 7-minute walk on a highly illuminated, LED-lit street side, patrolled by your on-site courtesy officer. Now, not only did you satisfy her need for safety, but also the need for convenience, being right next to her classes. Maybe the star athlete of the Hockey Club has a lot of gear he has to drag home every day, and he needs a place to store it. Conveniently, your floor plans offer massive walk-in closets that have more than enough space to accommodate all of his hockey equipment.

The definition of value is to consider something as important or worth having. Take the time to sit down and really get to know your lead and identify what their true need is. Then, you can take that information and apply it to every amenity you have. The secret to executing the perfect tour of your community is to forget about your community all together. Your tour is no longer about the property; it is about the person on the other side of the table. Now, you can treat this tour like everyone else does, and give your lead the watered down, standard tap version of your tour, or you can take the time to create value for your lead, and infuse every minute of your tour with a flavor that best fits their pallet, and leaves them with the experience of a lifetime. It is entirely up to you, but this is how you win!

Rip the Script

Giving a tour can be very complex because there are many layers that make it up, but that doesn't necessarily mean it has to be difficult. People overthink it! Here's the key: Don't be an asshole; think about the other person, and actually care. That's it. Too often, people over complicate things, like how long should my tour be? Should I show them all the amenities or just the model? Is this lead even qualified to live in my community? I don't want to waste my time if they're not going to sign here anyway. The only real question you should be asking is, *what is your intent?* Is this just about signing another lease, or do you truly care about the wellbeing of your lead? Most people will shrug their shoulders and say, *"The lease."* You don't really know the lead, so you could give a shit about their wellbeing, right? If this is your mindset, you will lose.

Think for a moment; why is your lead in your leasing office in the first place? Look at your target audience—an audience that has been wildly influenced by an uproar in technological advancements. We have grown up in a world of instant gratification. If you want to go shopping for something, you pull up Amazon Prime, click, and it's in your mailbox in two days. Hungry? Great! You don't have to eat out anymore; Uber Eats will bring it right to your doorstep. You don't even have to date anymore; all you have to do is pull out your cell phone and swipe right, for God's sake. This generation has adopted the model of instant gratification, and has applied it to every aspect of life, so why do you think leasing an apartment is any different? I'm sure you have a website, maybe even a virtual tour, and now we have online leasing available everywhere, unless you are still leasing in the barbaric times of the paper leasing. Ewwww... I just got shivers thinking about a paper lease. So, with all the resources and information at their fingertips, why is it that they are in your office wanting to take a tour in person?

Have you ever gone to a restaurant, and perused the menu up and down, only to find that everything suddenly looked good? The filet mignon, kale avocado salad, and chicken alfredo all sound mouthwatering. How do you decide which option to go with, when they are all equally viable? You spend another 10 minutes pretending to review other choices on the menu, but deep down inside, you know it is going to be one of the top three. Then, once you finally narrow it down and decide you're going with the filet, your server comes by to take your order, and the first thing you say is, "Excuse me, what would you suggest out of these three options?" Why do you do that, having already made up your mind, knowing you would be completely content with the steak? Why ask for other people's opinions? It is a self-imposed attempt to provide comfort to the most common objection that the majority of people have when faced with multiple options: the fear of making the wrong choice.

Your lead could have very easily made their decision from the comfort of their home, or they could've pulled out their iPhone while in line at Starbucks, and signed their lease without ever seeing your face. But the fact is, they are in your leasing office, in person, for one reason. They need your help. They need you to help justify why it is okay for them to live in your community, opposed to the next. They need your help to rationalize why your community is going to add the most value to their lifestyle. Most importantly, they want to hear your perspective to help provide comfort in their decision to go down the same path you did.

Your leads want to know about your experience. Why did you choose to live here? What are you most excited about? They may even want to know why you chose to live in this community, opposed to the next. This is why it is so important for your leasing team to be knowledgeable, not only about your community, but about your comps as well. It is also essential to make sure your leasing team is sold on your product. Why do you believe you have the best product in the market? What truly distinguishes your community from the next? Having a true affinity for your community will be the necessary fuel you will need when driving the lease home, even when you hit a road block. Let's face it; objections are inevitable. They are going to happen no matter what. So, when you do get asked those tough questions that weren't rehearsed in all your sales training, this is when your unadulterated belief in your product gets to shine. This is when you want to be versatile enough to rip the script and cut the bullshit. This is when you speak to your lead as a person, not as a robot reciting a rehearsed answer to an objection.

When you know your product enough, and know your market enough that you can be versatile in your tour, that is when you become dangerous. When you don't have to go down a script, and you can have fun, empathize, and really connect with your lead, that is when you realize that the apartment amenity won't matter anymore, because people buy people, not products.

If you don't know people, you will never know leasing. Empathy is the secret sauce. It should not be a question of whether or not this tour is going to turn into a lease, or how much commission you can gain from it. Think less about how you can profit from the transaction, and think more about how you can add value to your lead's life. Your intent should be to make yourself a resource, instead of a sales pitch.

If you master the art of empathy, you will close more deals. Speaking of closing—although I mentioned building rapport and creating an experience are the most important part of a tour—closing is the most important aspect of the leasing process. You can completely dominate a tour, but if you don't close, it means nothing. Closing is so important that it deserves a chapter of its own.

CHAPTER 6

S@#$ or Get Off the Pot

Hitch Leasing Principle on Closing

"You cannot use what you do not have. So, if you're shy, be shy. If you're outgoing, be outgoing... She may not want the whole truth, but she does want the real you."

It was back in 2013, when I talked myself into an entry level sales manager position, with Campus Crest Communities. I was 100% in charge of everything sales related at the property level, but I knew jack shit about sales. How I was qualified for this position? I still ask myself that question today. I had no previous manager experience. The only sales experience I had prior was that of my younger entrepreneurial self and the side hustles I had established to make money, like the dollar store candy bars I used to flip outside of the local Trader Joes, for $5 a pop. In my opinion, the only thing that made me even remotely qualified for this position was my year of community assistant experience, which I had gained from working at that same property 3 years prior, during my sophomore year in college. I learned, later, about a lingering rumor that the property I was hired at was an opportunity project, which meant it was prospectively going to sell, and they needed a sales manager on the books, as having a full staff would make it more marketable. I am still unsure of the validity of that rumor, but it did make sense at the time. The previous sales manager had taken a position in law enforcement, pursuing his dream, which left the property completely without management. The property was bleeding out and was in desperate need of help. Thus, the opportunity was up for grabs. You know what they say: "Luck is what happens when preparation meets opportunity." I am not sure how prepared I was for what would happen next, but I would definitely call it luck. Whether it was opportune timing or upper management's ability to see potential in me, the results were the same: They took a chance on me.

Knowing they took a shot in the dark on me, and according to all conventional hiring standards, I should not be in my position, I knew I had a very small window to prove my worth. So, immediately, I fully immersed in the leasing culture. I started learning all the leasing techniques offered company-wide. Any cool idea mentioned on our weekly calls, I implemented. I studied every sales book I could get my hands on. It would seem that I took a full curriculum on closing, as I think I learned every technique, from A–Z. I practically worshiped the movie, *The Wolf of Wall Street*, partly because of sales but mostly because it was awesome. Nonetheless, everything I learned, I attempted to apply to leasing apartments, yet nothing worked. I couldn't close a deal for the life of me. How was I supposed to teach a team of salespeople how to sell, if I couldn't close a deal my damn self?

So, I did the only thing I could think to do. I studied more, and practiced more closing techniques, and adopted the world renowned idiom, *Always be closing*. But my results were the same: failure after failure, over and over again. Everything I once knew to be true was coming to light. I wasn't cut out to be a salesperson, and I damn sure wasn't ready to be a manager. I would guess I was only about 2 months into the job at this point, and my self-esteem was at an all-time low; not to mention I was on yet another weekly under-performing conference call, where my area sales manager drilled me with question after question, in front of all the company bigwigs, to witness the hazing. Every week, I felt like we were playing a victory-less game of Jeopardy. "What are we doing to drive traffic? How many leases can you sign this week? What are we going to do to get out of the red?" I felt the urge to say, "What is, I don't fucking know, for $500?" But I knew that would only fast track my demise. I was a fish out of water, and honestly had no clue what to do.

In the coming weeks, my area sales manager, accompanied by a team of corporate employees, came to my office and completely wiped everything clean. All pictures of former staff, which we kept as a wall of fame, were trashed. Pictures of current staff were stuck underneath the reception desk—because, of course, it was the pictures on the walls that were hindering our leasing velocity. They redesigned our entire office, and completely drained all the culture out of the place, in a matter of 3 days. Then, once all the damage was done, she and I finally sat down and had a conversation to discuss my performance. I call it a conversation, but it was more so her chance to rip me a new one in person, instead of over the phone. In short, raw and uncensored, she basically told me that I was dispensable, and *"if you don't want to do your job, I will find somebody else who will."*

That was it. I met my breaking point. Facing myself in an internal game of tug of war, I was debating whether I should tell her to fuck off, or maintain my composure so I could keep my job. Fortunately, I chose the latter. How was she going to welcome me as a brand new sales manager, with no experience in property management, to this failing property, provide very minimal training, and expect me to turn it all around in less than 3 months' time? The property had a tarnished reputation, and it was known as the party apartment; not to mention the community's current occupancy was extremely low, so signing renewals alone just wouldn't cut it. She knew we were completely fighting an uphill battle, and expected me to turn this shithole around, after the countless managers before me who couldn't. I vented to a friend who currently worked as a roving sales manager for our corporate team, and I told her, "Fuck it! I give up. I feel like every time I talk to my area sales manager, I am on trial, or as if every conversation was an exam that I'm doomed to fail. I've done all I know how to do, and everything they have taught me. I'm done. If they are going to fire me, they are going to let me go knowing I did my very best, my way, because their way isn't working." That night, I went out for a drink to clear my mind and reset for tomorrow.

The following morning, I went in to the office, only to find a surprise. An unfamiliar face welcomed me and said, "Dude, you remember you told me to come check this place out last night? Well, here I am!" Fumbling to recall us ever meeting, let alone talking about apartments, I simply responded with the first thing that came to mind. "Oh, yeah!" I said hesitantly. "Nice to see you again, man! Let me show you around." I proceeded to give him the most informal, unprofessional tour I have ever given in my life. We sat down and talked about last night's drunken fiascos, talked about the sketchy apartment he lives in now, and discussed all the hot girls he noticed since he was on site. We talked, laughed, and completely bro'd out the entire tour. This tour lasted 30 minutes before even discussing an application. And yes, you guessed it… he signed his lease right on the spot!

But what was the difference? What happened this time that I lacked before when I was trying do all the standard sales techniques I had studied? The only thing I changed was me. Instead of focusing on being the next Jordan

Belfort, I created value by simply being myself. When we were able to connect on a level beyond sales person to consumer, the tour became fun instead of a task. I knew how to listen to his discontentment, create common ground, and simply make him feel good about himself, and that was enough—no fancy closing trick, just old fashioned authenticity. That year would turn out to be the catalyst for a series of the most record-breaking years the property had ever seen, and still goes down as some of the most epic years to this day.

Simon Sinek describes this idea as his *Golden Circle theory*, saying people don't buy what you do; they buy why you do it. David Simnick amended this idea by saying, *"It is true that people don't buy what you do; they buy why you do it. However, they only buy the why if it is authentic."* No matter what product you are selling, despite your proximity to campus or how big your pool is, YOU are your property's number one amenity. Yes, having a dynamic amenity package may help, or being the value add option will put you at an advantage to the price conscious, but at the end of the day, the greatest value you can add to a property is yourself."

I think Ben Baldanza, *former CEO of Spirit Airlines,* said it best when he compared Spirit Airlines to the fast food giant, McDonalds, saying, *"No one goes into McDonald's and is surprised they don't see filet mignon on the menu. Right?"* He suggested, *"So, when they come to Spirit, they know what they're getting."* We live in a world where everyone has something to sell, and they all have different tactics or closing techniques they implement to drive that sell: the Direct Close, the Assumptive Close, the Time Crunch Close, and the list goes on. The truth is, that lead has probably had 4 tours today, and they all said the same shit: "Spots are filling up fast, sign today!" So, I apologize if you were looking to learn a new earth shattering closing tactic, in this chapter, that would vastly change your leasing velocity overnight. There are libraries full of books that can teach you closing techniques. Unfortunately, this isn't one of them. The tactic I want to sell you on is one that is old as time but often gets overshadowed by the newest, most seller convenient ways to close. I want to sell you on being you.

Our sixth Hitch Leasing Principle for Closing is, *"You cannot use what you do not have. So, if you're shy, be shy. If you're outgoing, be outgoing... She may not want the whole truth, but she does want the real you."* The real you is the number one commodity you have at your community: your ability to laugh, relate, connect with people, and build a sense of community. That will outweigh any amenity you or your market has. Remember, when you put on an act and try to be something or somebody else you're not, you complete destroy your chances of connecting with your lead. So, do me a favor and graduate from the overly common phrase: "Always be closing." Although it is true that closing is a process, if you want to lease up your community, increase your velocity, and build a culture of residents that want to renew repeatedly, adopt the only closing strategy that matters: "Always be authentic."

No Means Yes, Sometimes

Dopamine is a neutron transmitter in our bodies, which is responsible for communicating signals in between the neurons in our brains. But what does that mean? This is a chemical release in our bodies that is responsible for our feeling of happiness, motivation, concentration, etc. There are many ways that dopamine is released, but one that we meet often is through feelings of affirmation. You just closed on a deal! You just got a promotion! You just landed a date with the person of your dreams! Immediately, that feeling of elation on the other side of an achievement, causes a release of dopamine, making us want to revisit, in some form, that high, over and over again. Sound familiar? That's because it is. Dopamine is also released by consuming alcohol or other substances that make us feel good. Hence, it is how people become alcoholics or develop addictions to other substances. My point is, people have become almost physically addicted to the very elation we get on the other side of affirmation. People are addicted to "Yes."

Think about it; as a young child going through the toy store with their parents, what is the first thing they do as soon as they get there? They ask for the first toy in sight. "Mom! Pleeeeeease, can I have it?" Mom agrees; and the kids scream "yes!" Only to play with said toy for maybe 15 minutes before losing interest and reverting back to torturing your poor dog, dragging it by the tail for entertainment. As a teenager who has been conditioned to get good grades and do their chores in order to get a weekly allowance, what is the first thing they say at the sight of an A+? "Yes!" Then they go piss all their earnings away on new video games. Even as adults, we will put it all on the line, our full egos completely exposed and vulnerable in front of all of our friends and family, to ask one simple question, "Will you marry me?" Then, when your significant other says yes, you celebrate with a year full of *Yes!* Yes to the dress. Will you be my best man? Yes! Will you be my maid of honor? Yes! We live for these moments—the moments that allow us to scream, "Yes!" There are even sales mirror agreement theories that prove this to be an effective closing strategy. The more times you can get someone to yes through confirmation, we assume that they will commit with a yes at the end of the sales pitch.

Leasing agents are not exempt from this yes addiction in the leasing space. In fact, you are probably amongst the most obsessed when it comes to getting a yes out of your leads; hence why you always ask questions like, "Are you available to meet for your tour today? Are you ready to secure your top floor unit?" We get a natural high off of getting our leads to say yes and commit to signing a lease. Now, I am not saying that the *yes theory* is ineffective; hell, I have and still use this form of rhetoric today. However, have you ever given any thought to what might happen if you focused on utilizing the power of the word, *no*, instead?

Hear me out. We live in a world where our consumer

is demanding more transparency. When it comes to food, people buy free range or organic chicken, even at a higher price point, in fear of what brands are doing to process their food. When it comes to making any online purchase, the first thing you look at is the reviews. Why? Because the consumer knows that no brand is going to tell you they have a shitty product, but a previous client will keep it real on a review. In leasing, this is the same mindset many of our leads come in with. Your lead was not born yesterday, and they understand the concept of sales. Oftentimes, they come in, apprehensive at the idea that this is their first time leasing an apartment, and some sleazy salesman is going to try to reach into their pockets. "I am not signing anything today; I am just here to weigh out my options." And every time you attempt to gain their confirmation, you actually activate the little voice in their head that is asking, "What is he up to?" or, "I know there is a catch somewhere. Don't trust him." All the while, that little voice in your lead's head is their number one distraction, completely adulterating their attention to the amazing tour that you are giving.

Instead of focusing all of your attention on trying to manipulate your lead into saying yes, try seeing this engagement through the eyes of your prospect, with empathy. During your tour, dive deeper into why your lead actually needs your product. Pay attention to the buy signs that really get them excited. Then figure out what is the true root cause of their apprehension. Once you have established this emotional connection, use this information to appeal to the number one objection every lead has: the fear of making the wrong decision. Do this by using the power of *No*.

Christopher Voss, *American businessman and former FBI negotiator*, describes this phenomenon as the rhetoric Ronald Reagan used in his "Are You Better Off?" speech, to win over the hearts of America in his elections. It was just as powerful then as it is today, almost 40 years later. Voss goes further to say that the term, *no*, instills a sense of protection, safety, and security—all the things that *yes* does not; hence, the concept of buyer's remorse. Obviously, this doesn't happen to everybody, as some people are ecstatic to have signed their lease at your community. But think about those hard sells that you have to really convince that your community is the perfect home for them. They may say *yes* now, but something in your stomach may tell you it isn't right. Then they walk out with their head hanging low, wondering if they made the right decision, and you leave with a pit in your stomach, praying they didn't read the part of the contract about the 72-hour cancellation clause.

Now, imagine if you said something like this: "Samantha, I know you said your space and price were most important to you in your next home. You need a place that not only accommodates you but also accepts your puppy, Chewy. Considering all we went over today, including our massive, pet friendly townhomes with the biggest square footage in town, the brand new dog park, perfect for Chewy to run free, and the amazing special we have right now, saving you over $1,000, personally I think this is the perfect home for you and your fur baby. But the question is, with all things considered, is this really a deal you can afford to miss out on?" It is amazing the amount of things people will say *no* to, to protect themselves from the opposition. My guess is that her mind would immediately do what our minds are designed to do, and go on the defense. But this time, Samantha's mind won't be protecting her from her fear of whether or not she made the right choice, but rather her fear of missing out on a deal of a life time.

The number one secret to closing is: there isn't one. There is no such thing as a secret sauce to close on every deal. The goal of closing is not to use some Jedi mind trick bullshit to manipulate your lead into making an impulse decision. Your goal is to create so much value in your product that the fear of missing out on this opportunity alone will be the driving force for your lead's decision. Challenge yourself to get addicted to empathy. See your community through the eyes of your prospect, and along your tour, take them to Nirvana. The pure fulfillment that you will meet, merely from servicing others, I guarantee will be the best high you've ever been on.

Dealing with Objections

Dealing with objections is bullshit! I remember these words vividly. Early in my property management career, I attended a sales seminar, hoping to better equip myself with new techniques; and a speaker opened his segment with that statement. It really stuck with me because it was shocking. His stance defied all conventional wisdom about everything I had come to learn about handling objections, and frankly, it went against everything I had been teaching my staff up to that point. Charismatically, he continued making his claim by saying if you create enough value in your product, you should never have to deal with an objection. Now, I agree, there is much validity in this statement. The more value you can create for your lead, the more inclined they are going to be to lease with you. However, I have learned over the years that there are three things in life you cannot escape, no matter how hard you try: death, taxes, and objections. That's just facts; people will always have their objections—it's their job to do this.

Ben Affleck, as Jim Young, in his 2000 film, *Boiler Room*, stated in his famous *Always Be Closing* speech, *"There is no such thing as a no-sale call. A sale is made on every call you make. Either you sell the client some stock, or he sells you a reason he can't. Either way, a sale is made. The only question is, who is gonna close? You or him? Now, be relentless ..."* Now, no matter your opinion how great the film was, there is much validity to this statement when it comes to apartment leasing. Very few times does your lead ever come into your community with their mind already made up that they are going to live there. More often, they come in with their mind already made up that they are not signing anything that day, or for one reason or another, they are going to postpone making a decision. So as much as it is your job to sell them on how amazing living at your community is going to be, their job is to sell you on why they don't need your apartment right now. Either way, a sale is being made. The difference is that we identify their sales pitch as an objection.

The truth is that objections are part of the process. Honestly, if you successfully guide your lead through this leasing process without meeting some form of an objection, you should be surprised. The problem is, too often, leasing agents see this in reverse. You go out and give your best tour, close with your best pitch, and when the lead objects, your eyes light up like a deer in the head lights. You freeze, heart racing at 100 miles per hour, while you contemplate what to do. Then, all at once, you sift through your library of preloaded rebuttals that you practiced during your objection training, find one that fits, then throw it out like a Hail Mary in 4th quarter, praying that your lead catches it. But just like in football, depending on the Hail Mary, *all the time* is a failing formula.

Consider this: about 85% of leasing agents come in with no prior sales experience. In the student housing space, you may be lucky if they come in with work experience at all, let alone a sales job. And no, selling coffee at Starbucks doesn't count. So, to expect your leasing agent to master the best ways to deal with objections, without proper training, is not practical. The trick to dealing with objections is less about the objection itself, and more about dealing with your self-confidence.

When it comes down to signing leases, it all boils down

to the leasing agent with the most swag. How confident are you in what you are selling? The reason why people are so scared of objections is not about the objection; it's more about how confident your leasing agent is in dealing with that pressure. Eighty percent of all leasing agents only ask for the sale one time after the tour, and it sounds like: "So… what do you think? Want to start an application today?" Not even the agent believes that shit is going to work. Another 10% are willing to ask for the sale once, deal with the objection that follows, then go for the sale a second or third time. That leaves the last 10% to be the sharks: the ones that want to win; the leasing agents that will go the extra mile and do everything that it takes to sign a lease. They will hop on FaceTime with Mom and Dad if they believe it all seems too good to be true, and they will drive to the residents halls to meet their friends, if they are the decision makers. That's the level of confidence your leasing agents need to possess.

Coming up with fun objection trainings is great: objection speed dating, objection Jenga, and so on and so forth. But if you don't focus on instilling confidence in your team, they will never feel comfortable when an objection presents itself. Some may even argue that you cannot teach self-confidence, and that you have to hire for the shark mentality, and just point them in the direction to feed. Either way, shift your focus from dealing with objection, and focus more on dealing with self-confidence; but that is going to require a shift in how you look at objections overall. Objections are not obstacles; they are opportunities.

When you hear an objection, you should get excited! You should be doing cartwheels in your head! Obviously, you don't want to show this to your lead, but you should identify an objection as another buy sign. This means your lead is actually considering living in your community. This means you have almost won them over; they just have a few small details that may be standing in their way of making a decision. But now you have the opportunity to isolate whatever it is that is causing that hesitation, and instill your confidence in them by giving them a solution.

I said it before, and I will repeat it over again, because it's true: To be successful in dealing with objection, just like anything else, it is 80% psychological and 20% technical. If you minimize the idea of an objection from some type of massive hurdle that is preventing you from signing a lease, and see it instead as an opportunity to be a resource to your lead, you will realize that objections are not as bad as they seem. You can do all the rebuttal trainings, and study all the objection flash cards you want, but if you don't shift your mindset and become more confident in your approach, it will be all for not.

So, I did take something from that seminar that is as true today as it was then. Dealing with objections is bullshit. But not because you can avoid them—that is a little ambitious—but because the term, *objections*, itself, is the bullshit. Instead, practice dealing with self-confidence, so when your team does get asked those tough questions that seem like a cloud that swept in on your parade, your mere confidence alone will leave you dancing in the rain.

Stop Selling! Start Serving!

Okay, now that you know how to deal with external objections, how do you master dealing with those internally—the objections often found among your own leasing team? Let's face it; it is nearly impossible to sell a product that you're not sold on yourself, unless you're just a master bullshitter. So how do you deal with a team who is not mentally bought in? In most cases, I would say to hell with it. If that leasing agent is cancer to your productivity, then it's time for you to be chemo. Get them out as early as possible, before their effect on the team's morale becomes terminal. However, in other cases, where you have a really strong team member that simply needs a change in perspective, it may require what Tony Robbins would call a *2-millimeter shift*. This is the theory that describes the small, incremental changes that can be made in order to make a massive impact on your business, or in this case, your ability to close leases.

Much like dealing with external objections, one of the biggest hurdles you will come across with your staff is their lack of self-confidence. However, this time it's not necessarily in their ability to respond to a prospect's objection, but more in their ability to be a salesperson all together. Most leasing agents will come into this position expecting this job to be a front desk job, where they sit around for 5 hours pushing papers, logging packages, and simply passing time to collect a paycheck, until they get the occasional customer who walks in, and they just show them around the community. Reality check! Working in leasing is a sales position, and you have to approach it as such. Unfortunately, when your leasing agents are faced with this reality, they quickly start to break down, and their insecurity starts to surface. "I didn't sign up to be a salesperson," they proclaim, or go as far as saying, "Sales is not for me; I was interested in the administration side of the business."

I encountered a situation similar to this when I was on a site visit, training one of the leasing teams in my portfolio on outreach marketing. I posed a question to the audience: "What are some of the greatest hurdles you encounter when attempting to market?" Immediately, I saw a hand raise to the sky, from my peripherals. I slowly turned my head to the right, and noticed a gentleman by the name of Alex, eager to speak, like he had been waiting to make this point all night. I signaled him to stand and tell us about his experience. Enthusiastically, he stood up and said, "Well, nobody approaches us while we are tabling. They always feel like we are trying to sell them something, and nobody likes to be sold to. This is frustrating because I hate being treated like a salesperson. This is why I was hesitant to take on a sales job in the first place." His voice progressively lowered in tone, exposing his discontentment with the idea all together. He went further to say, "The University Connection program always has people at their table, because they are actually giving students stuff, not trying to sell them something."

Acknowledging his concerns, and validating his right

to feel the way he does, I probed a little further to see what the University Connections organization was giving away that really made their product stand out. He went on to tell me, "They offer students opportunities. All the student has to do is sign up with the program, and they get connected with opportunities." Immediately, I understood what was going on. He was able to create a full motion picture in my head of what happens when he is outreach marketing, simply with those few words. He personally perceived marketing his property as more of an inconvenience to prospects, rather than an opportunity. It's not necessarily the lead; he himself was not bought in. I took this platform as an opportunity of my own to educate him and his peers in hopes of shifting the way they perceived sales.

"Everything is a sales campaign," I implored to my trainee audience, much like I will impress upon you. No matter how massive the brick and mortar, or how small the internet startup, everything is a sales campaign. Some may wrap it up in an opportunity bow, and deliver it that way, or they may keep it raw and direct, with an easily detectible sales pitch. But either way, it is still sales. Hell, even in a job interview, you must position yourself as the product, and sell yourself to your intended employer, as the consumer. Everywhere you go, and in just about everything you do, someone is selling something. This may be the unpopular stance to many of you, but I promise you it's real. I will die on this hill knowing that as long you are asking or otherwise suggesting that someone buy into your ideological framework, you are selling — whether that be a product or a perspective, it's sales.

The problem is, too often, people view sales as the process of some conniving, manipulating, untrustworthy scumbag forcefully shoving a product down the throat of an averse buyer. Naturally, *good* people and their moral compass steer away from the practice, and develop a negative disposition for the concept overall. In reality, sales is nothing more than basic level human to human interaction—a concept of engaging in interpersonal communication and developing common ground. Then, once you have established such rapport, identify a need that person may have, and position yourself as a resource to fulfill their void. That's it! A salesperson would be better seen as a facilitator of conversation. Simply because you cannot make someone buy anything against their will, all you can do is ask a series of stimulating questions, leading you both to a mutually agreed upon solution to a previously disclosed problem.

Therefore, if you are constantly thinking about the consumer, and wondering how you can help solve their problems, then every conversation you have should sound like an *opportunity*, right? This is the key ingredient Alex was missing—the 2-millimeter shift that could alter his method of tabling, from feeling like a nuisance to showing prospects that he, too, is an opportunity. It may not be an internship or a study abroad trip, but it is the opportunity to live in the best community in town! If that's not an opportunity, I don't know what is! People don't need to study Liberal Arts in fucking Guam. They do so by choice.

However, they do need a place to live, and to do so, without compromising their standard of living, that's one hell of an opportunity. However, you have to truly believe it, and know your audience enough to articulate how important this really is.

This was another flaw in Alex's approach: He didn't know his audience. He was tabling in the middle of November, in an area on campus highly saturated with juniors and seniors who are, 1) probably more concerned with getting their shit together for life after college right now, or 2) probably just moved in to their current apartment and haven't even made plans for lunch today, let alone where they are going to live next year. So I asked the group where they were seeing the most new traffic coming from this season. They all agreed that the freshman and sophomore demographic was most prominent, as they were most discontent with their current housing. "That's great!" I replied. "If that is the bulk of your traffic, and those are the people who are signing the most leases right now, wouldn't you like to see more of those leads in your pipeline?" I questioned, then went forward to suggest different targeting strategies to attract more people from that exact audience.

This is a strategy the late Chet Holmes, *Author and Fortune 500 business advisor of sales and marketing,* would call the *Best Buyer Strategy*: a concept of identifying your ideal buyer, targeting them, and doing something special that will attract more buyers just like them. If you notice a trend of leases coming in from freshmen living in the stratum resident hall, then focus your attention on attracting more student in stratum. Instead of tabling in front of the student union building, why not flyer in front of the most popular freshman lounge area, or table by the on-campus dining centers? If your product is in a location that is most appealing to Greeks, and your market has a really large Greek live-out community, then why not strategically find a way to appeal to them? Sponsor their grilled cheese sandwich, philanthropy event for autism awareness, or sponsor their Mom's weekend event by buying their t-shirts. Whatever it is, identify your best buyer, and market to them consistently. That is the key: consistency. Driving an audience does not happen overnight. It takes time. That is all the University Connection program did. They found their ideal buyer and used what they knew about them to motivate them to act.

Now that you have identified your target audience, and know their interest, position yourself as more of a resource than a sales pitch. That's the easiest way to get over the negative feeling of being considered a salesperson. Add more value to the product through educational based sales. Simply know what your buyer needs to know in order to motivate them to buy your product. For instance, I was managing a new development apartment in California, when I met a very inquisitive parent while marketing during a university tour. She informed me that her son had already signed up for housing in the residence halls for the upcoming year, but they were still waiting on confirmation on whether or not he would get in. I cannot remember the placement she had mentioned they were on the waitlist, but I do remember it was absurd!

I had managed another new development the year prior, in the same market, and had insight on the on-campus housing trends. With this knowledge, I simply took it as an opportunity to educate her. Little did she know, this year, her son was part of a record breaking year for the amount of freshmen accepted in the university's history. However, even with last year's freshman enrollment numbers alone, on-campus housing was oversaturated. Even after doubling occupancy in many single rooms to further accommodate the student capacity, the university still had to turn away roughly 375 students to find housing elsewhere; not to mention, notice was not offered to the families affected by this until mid-July, and they were expected to start their semester less than a month later. Essentially, all of these families were up shit creek without a paddle. Students ended up paying inflated rates for the dumps they had to live in, and in bad neighborhoods, all because they believed in a waitlist and a promise that never came true. I then implored her to just come look at my community, with her new found knowledge. Later that day, the family ended up coming by to visit, signed a lease, and invited 3 other roommates to do the same. All because I was able to offer her a little education, I essentially added more value to our community, in the eyes of my consumer.

Sales does not have to be complicated. If you do the same simple, tactical things everyone else does, you're going to get what everyone else gets, and you'll be treated accordingly. However, if you take the time to identify who your best buyer is, and figure out what they need to know to motivate them to make a decision, you will position yourself to be more of a resource than an inconvenience. The value you add through the education you provide will outweigh any promotion you can throw their way. Your lead won't just be ecstatic to sign a lease with you; they will feel like they just closed on the opportunity of a lifetime.

Emulate Your Favorite Restaurant

Price does not close deals; value does. If you are the value add option in the market, great! Be the best added value to your consumer that you can possibly be. If you're the brand new premiere option in the market, then hell, be the premiere option, and own it. Sure, you're not going to be for everyone, but you will be everything to those in your target audience. Price, promotions, concessions, and incentives are all factors, no doubt, but they are not everything. It's no secret that everyone wants to secure the best deal, but that deal is not always measured by the size of the gift card you are giving away, or you being $20 cheaper than your competition. If your worth is defined by the concession you give a student to sign a lease, then you are in trouble, my friend. Your community's true worth is not in the promotion used to attract your consumer, but it is in the value you create in your product.

When it comes to creating value, meditate on the idea

of your favorite restaurant. No, I'm not talking about fast food. I'm talking about the real shit. However, if you do identify your property as the fast food option in this analogy, be the Chick-fil-A of fast food, and don't settle for Burger King or Arby's. You're better than that. I'm talking about the restaurant you went to for your last birthday, or the date you went on to celebrate your last anniversary. These are the restaurants who have figured it out.

Think for a moment about the last time you went out and had a really nice dinner, and walk yourself through that experience. Hone in on that moment and see if you share any similarities, while I tell you about mine. It was Valentine's Day, or rather, the day prior. My fiancé and I decided to celebrate a day early to avoid the inevitable madness of the restaurant industry, in Houston, TX, on Valentine's Day. So, we got all dressed up, and we went to a restaurant called Eddie V's Prime Seafood. Neither of us had ever been, but it had been highly recommended by some of my colleagues, so we decided to give it a try.

Instantaneously, an existential feeling of elegance intoxicated us as soon as we stepped foot into the restaurant. The ambiance was set by the perfectly dimmed lights beaming from the luxury chandeliers, dreamily complimented by the candles dressing each table; not to mention the soothing sound of smooth, live jazz playing from the far end of the room. Immediately, the first impression alone laid the foundation for the unparalleled experience we would soon come to meet.

After waiting in a surprisingly short line, we

approached the receptionist desk and confirmed our reservation. "Welcome, Mr. Butler," she greeted, and then hastily escorted us to our table. Once seated, we realized that we were placed in a booth that would easily accommodate six or more guests, but we were only a party of two. Moments later, we were welcomed by our attendant: "Is this the Butler party?" he questioned, and then introduced himself as James, and informed us he would be taking care of us that evening. Noticing a slight discomfort from my fiancé and me, James asked, "Is there anything I can do for you before we dive into the menu?" When we requested to move just a few tables down to an open assignment better fit to accommodate two, James immediately reacted as if we were the only couple in the room.

Now that we were comfortable, James returned to our newly assigned table and continued to build rapport with us. He welcomed us with a complimentary glass of NV Moet and Chandon Nectar Imperial Rose Champagne. We joked, laughed, and were having a blast, all before even having a chance to look at the menu. Then, to our surprise, James had quickly unearthed that we were celebrating Valentine's Day early, so he went further to invest in our experience by bringing a handful of rose pedals to dress the center of our table. The look on my fiancé's face would only come second to the day I proposed in the first place. James was working the room, and we loved every moment of it.

Finally, after a thorough description of the menu, and

very motivating suggestions of top menu items, we ordered our food and it was time to eat. I ordered a seared Chilean sea bass, topped with king crab that was drowned in butter to perfection. My fiancé ordered a medium-rare, 22 oz., prime bone-in, ribeye steak, so big that I was convinced she ordered the whole cow. We coupled this with a side of truffle mac and cheese, along with roasted spinach. Talk about food porn at its finest. I will save you all the sexy details, but in short, the experience was orgasmic.

Eventually, we finished our meal and savored every last bite as if it were the first. Then, as if he hadn't done enough already, James came out and offered us a complimentary dessert, simply because we were great guests. Unfortunately, we had no room for the sweet treat, but he put the cherry on top in another way. When James delivered our check, he coupled it with an individual, long-stemmed rose tied to baby's breath, and signaled to me to present it to my fiancé. This night could not have been any better. The atmosphere was second to none, our attendant didn't miss a beat with his customer service, and the overall experience was unbelievable, and definitely made for a memorable Valentine's Day eve. So when I reviewed my bill to find a $180 ticket price, there was no question that this night was well worth the money. Of course, this bill included our appetizers and drinks as well, but the experience alone was priceless, so much so that not only was I okay with paying the $180 bill, but I left James a $40 tip!

Now, if I would have called Eddie V's prior to our visit and asked how much my meal would be, and had they responded that it would cost $180, I would have slammed the phone in the receptionist's face. And we would have spent Valentine's Day at Applebee's. However, having the opportunity to fully immerse in the experience of the restaurant, interact with the people that make up the culture, taste the unprecedented delicacies of the food, and witness the pure expression of satisfaction on my fiancé face, not only was I willing to pay the ticket price, but I was willing to pay an additional 22%! Why? Because the value James created outweighed the price that I was charged.

When value outweighs the price, the price is no longer the value. This is where many go wrong. You print out rate sheets before your tours, or you answer the phone and by default tell the lead the rates and promotions within seconds of conversing with them. Essentially, you're sliding your lead the ticket before they can enjoy the meal. They haven't even seen your property or had the opportunity to experience your culture, and you have already started talking about rates and promotions. Even worse is when a lead puts in an online inquiry, and the first line of your template email response is your rates and the great concession that you're using to bribe them into a lease. Now what happens when your rates exceed their intended budget? You lose that lead in the first sentence of your email.

Now, some may argue that if your community is out of your lead's budget, they wouldn't have committed anyway. However, I would implore that whenever someone says that a product is too expensive, that doesn't necessarily mean they don't have enough money to pay for it. That means they have not associated enough value to the product to justify the spend. You just haven't made it meaningful enough yet. If you can prove your product is worth the ROI, then your lead will be more willing to eat the additional cost. But by prematurely offering your rates before creating values, you cut all chances of making your claim later. Price and promotions are not the silver bullet. In certain mediums, like selective internet listing sites or social advertisements, if your price and promotions are the best in the market, they can be great for driving traffic. However, once your lead is in the office, or you have them on the phone, price should be the least of your concerns. You should be more focused on the amount of value you can add to your prospective buyer.

Students, just like the rest of us, are relatively simple. They have a certain set of values that stand true no matter what university. They value education, at least, theoretically, we can assume so. They value experience because, if not, they probably could be taking the same courses online, or at the local community college. They value their networks and social relationships they cultivate. The list goes on. However, the number one value that is becoming more and more prevalent to everyone, especially as the advertising landscape becomes more competitive, is time.

After maybe the second or third community your lead

looks into on their apartment search, all the options start to look alike. Your lead goes on a tour, and the leasing agent shows them amenity after amenity, all of which show a striking resemblance to the last community, but for one reason or another, that property is better than every other one, at least according to the leasing agent. Apartment searching is not fun. Fun is what your lead does on a Saturday night with all their friends, at a house party drinking, playing beer pong, and shooting the shit. Apartment searching can be very time intensive, cumbersome, and monotonous when dealing with your average leasing agents. That is partially why people procrastinate to actually go on the search, because they know it is going to demand a lot of time. Too often, leasing agents try their hardest to sell their property as the best product in the market, when really your lead only cares about which property is the best fit for them.

The bottom line is, if you want to add more value to your lead, you have to first value your lead. Take the time to get to know them and find their *why*. Figure out what is driving their decision, and use that to help motivate them. Quit using your concessions to define the worth of your community. Your community is worth the value you create. Create an experience for your lead like no other, which will truly distinguish your property from any other in market. Add value to your prospect, beyond your rates and current promotions. Then, once they are all full on the consummate experience you have cast, and have tasted the brilliant flavor of your community's culture, the concessions that you offer will simply be the dessert to an otherwise exceptional meal. Then, when there is nothing left to do but slide your lead the check, I can not only guarantee you will close the deal, but the same-day close is going to tell you whether or not you got the tip. But that is all determined by how you stress urgency.

Stressing Urgency

Nothing would get done if it weren't for the last minute. Without a doubt, people are always going to want to get things done on their own time, when they are most convenient. If you leave it up to your lead, they will always want to take as much time as possible to *think* about the decision of whether or not they want to live in your community. But let's be honest; there are very few decisions in life that require you to *think* that long and hard, if you really put your mind to it. "Okay, we need two weeks to really think about this decision." When was the last time you thought about anything for 2 full weeks? I mean, really sat down and thought about any one thing for 2 weeks' time. That's 14 days, or 336 hours, or 20,160 minutes. Really? I would argue that many of you would agree that you have never spent that much consecutive time thinking about any one thing. There are some high priority, more life altering decisions that demand more thought than others. For instance, major investments, career changes, emotional disputes, business development decisions, marriage, etc. But hell, not 2 consecutive weeks.

I think it took me more time to muster up the courage to propose than it did for me to decide that my wife-to- be is the one I want to spend the rest of my life with. It's not necessarily the time that your lead needs to make a decision; it is more so the urgency they need to help get them there.

The reasons why deadlines exist in the first place is to associate a sense of value to the task at hand, make it more of a priority, and thus demand you complete said task in a timely manner. If not, things would never get done, especially the things that introduce stress into your life. Moving to a new home is one of the top 10 stressors any adult will meet in their lives, falling only behind death of a loved one, and divorce. So, naturally, your lead is going to want to put this off as long as possible. Unless there is a sense of urgency that requires your lead to prioritize signing their lease now versus later, they will always deprioritize it as something they will do when they "can get to it." This is the epitome of procrastination. I will say this again: Nothing would get done if it weren't for the last minute. As the leasing agent in this equation, it is your job to create that *last minute* by stressing urgency.

The concept of stressing urgency seems simple. Urge a level of importance to your lead by demanding swift action. It seems straight forward enough. However, it can be one of the hardest things to get your leasing team to do without providing enough perspective. You feel like stressing urgency is pushy, and it makes your leads uncomfortable. You don't want to be assertive toward them because if a similar situation like this happened to you, you would be uneasy. The truth is, your lead is already uneasy. They are facing an internal torment of not knowing where they are going to live next year. Remember, this is one of the greatest stressors one will face in their life. You have the solution to their problem, and because you are afraid of making them uncomfortable in that one moment, you are depriving them of the very resource they need that will save them many more. Your lack of urgency is further sentencing them to suffer with this question for another 2 weeks, until they finally do what we already know they were going to do all along: live in your community.

I will acknowledge in advance that this is going to contradict what I had said previously. The fact remains, the most common reason why people don't buy what you are selling is because they are uncomfortable. However, when it comes to stressing urgency, discomfort is part of the process. Discomfort inspires action. Think about it; if you were to walk into Bed, Bath and Beyond, and plop down on one of their massive, bean bag chairs, you could spread your arms out and pass out there for hours without a care in the world. That's because you're comfortable, and there is nothing driving you to move out of your comfort zone. However, if you ever lived in a dorm and had to sleep on those paper thin, twin-sized mattresses that remind you of what you would get if you were doing 25 to life in the state penitentiary, you wouldn't be able to wait to get the hell off of that thing! If not, your back is going to feel like you have someone's knee in it for the rest of the day. That's the same way stressing urgency works: If you allow your lead ample time to sit on this decision, they will do so for as long as you make it comfortable for them to do so. It is not until your lead risks facing the pain or the loss associated with missing out, that they will finally get up and act.

Fear of loss is more of a motivator to people than the opportunity to gain. So by stressing urgency, you are compelling your lead to make a decision sooner, because they will do anything to avoid the repercussions of the opposite. This is why creating value is so important. Urgency will only work if your product means something to the lead. Without meaning, your urgency is meaningless. You can't tell someone "we only have 3 spots left, so act fast," and expect them to do so if they don't give a damn about your apartments. It doesn't work like that. In order for urgency to work, you must have influence.

Many leasing agents are very one-dimensional. If you do stress urgency at all, you typically do so by stressing your limited availability in units or promotions. However, what happens when convenience is more of a priority than price? Or someone is more concerned with experience than they are with having your last top floor, 1-bedroom floor plan? Dr. Robert Cialdini, *Professor and author of "Influence: Science and Practice,"* has a really good grasp of the concept of influence, with his theory on the six principles of persuasion. I would like to briefly explore some of these, and how they can offer new ways you can influence your leads to make quicker decisions:

Reciprocity

This is the concept where people feel obligated to give back to people who have previously given to them. The most effective practice here is to give first, and without expectation. Then, based on basic human principle, your lead will be more inclined to do for you as you have done for them. Quid pro quo. For instance, if your lead is more concerned with convenience, and wants to live on the east side of the property, which is closest to the Business School, you could suggest, "Hey, Jared, I know you were really interested in this specific unit, as you want to easily access your classes. Although I am supposed to operate on a first-come, first-serve basis, today I can do this just for you. I will go to bat for you and make sure you get this particular unit, by putting it on hold so no one else can lease it, because I know how important it is for you." Theoretically, because you acknowledge the importance to Jared, and made his needs a priority, he will be more inclined to do the same for you.

Consistency or Commitment

This explains why it is typically easier to get your leads to sign a lease with you, if they have already completed an application previously. People are more inclined to continue doing the things that they have already started. People like to be consistent with what they have previously committed to. This level of commitment creates a sense of investment in your lead's mind, which gives them a certain stake in your community. Therefore, this process of getting your lead to commit to something small will lead them to committing to something greater later down the line. This is especially beneficial when you cannot secure the same day close. Urge your lead to at least complete the application so they will be more inclined to sign a lease soon after.

Consensus

When contemplating buying something you are unsure about, what is the first thing you do? Check out reviews? Ask a friend? Ask an advocate for their opinion? This is because there is a lot of truth to the old saying that the true leader is usually the first follower. In fear of isolation, nobody wants to be the first and only person to do something. That makes you look like a lonely quack job. And no one likes to be the only person left out who is not doing what the masses are doing. Therefore, people are more inclined to do what is socially accepted. This is how social trends are created. There is power in numbers, and seeing that many other people are doing it stresses urgency that your lead needs to do it as well. This is why social media can have such a major effect on your community's traffic. Even more effective is if you have an office full of people signing leases all at once; it will motivate other prospects to do the same.

Authority

People are more inclined to take advice or be influenced by people they see as credible or an expert in their field. The whole concept of authority is not necessarily rooted in what you know, but more so in who knows what you know. When you need legal advice, you are more inclined to listen to an attorney. When you want to lose weight, you will take advice from a personal trainer. Why? Because they are experts in their field. So now that your lead needs to find housing, and needs advice on the best opinion for them, position yourself as the expert in your market. If they want to go see other apartments, you should be able to articulate the difference of those other options, and explain why your community holds greater value. Your lead will see you as the expert, and be more inclined to listen to you. Then, once you tell them it's time to act fast, they will listen again, because they know that you know your shit.

Scarcity

Another tale, as old as time, is that we always want what we can't have. This is the idea that simply saying that living at your community is the best, is not good enough; you have to also express what the lead will miss out on if they choose not to. This is the most commonly used of the principles in the apartment leasing community. You will often hear people stating that their rates are increasing soon, or how they have very limited availability. This is designed to appeal to the innate fear that we all have of not being able to have the things that we want. By limiting the availability of your apartments, it creates more value to your lead; thus, it further entices them to make an immediate decision to avoid missing out.

Liking

Put simply, people don't buy products; they buy people. No doubt, your leads are more inclined to lease apartments that they like. However, they are more motivated to buy from people that they like. By establishing common ground, you are eliminating the idea of you vs. me, and establishing a culture of "we." This concept of oneness creates more justification for your lead to buy your product, and follow your influence.

You see, urgency does not have to always come in the form of scarcity, where you are threatening the loss of a promotion. This is a very effective tool indeed, but once you get to know your lead, you will no longer have to be one-dimensional. Conventional wisdom and over ambitious optimism in mankind may convince you to think that 2 weeks is a reasonable amount of time to consider all the variables included in the apartment search. However, we live in a time where people would use an app to take a shit if the technology existed, just so they could save time. People take shortcuts for just about everything, and the leasing process is no different.

People don't need two weeks to make a decision, and

by you giving it to them, you're doing your leads more of a disservice than you are servicing them. Stressing urgency does not mean being pushy; it means inducing a little discomfort to inspire action. Your lead wants to find a home, and right now they have an ever insidious problem they are facing that you have all the resources to solve. So don't be selfish—solve it. They deserve urgency, and it's up to you to give it to them.

I'm sure, as your new customers, they would have appreciated the service.

CHAPTER 7

All the Feels

HITCH LEASING PRINCIPLE #7: Hospitality

"What if fine isn't good enough…
What if I want extraordinary?"

Good customer service is not good enough. I know, this statement is not going to win the most popular vote award; however, let me explain. I had a very eye opening experience with the expectations of both the server and serviced when it comes to how we view customer service. In part, I would attribute my point of view on customer service to this event.

It was a typical Saturday evening, in Allendale, Michigan, and much like many obsessive managers like myself, I found any excuse to make my way back to the leasing office, even on my day off. It all started that morning when I decided to get up and take my routine run, followed by a binge read on the university stadium steps. Living just about a mile away from the property, I decided to take what I called the scenic route. Many of you probably wouldn't describe it with such elegance, but it led right back to our brand new leasing office, which was indeed a sight to see, all by itself. Finally, making it to the property, I thought to myself, "I'll just stop in for a minute to see how things are going," rationalizing my excuse to check on my leasing team. As we all know, everything is never perfect in student housing; there is always more work to be done. So, one thing led to the next, and before I knew it, what was intended to be just a minute turned into practically a full 8-hour shift. Needless to say, there wasn't very much reading done that day.

Eventually, I mustered up the self-discipline to tear myself away from the office, and decided to run my way back home. My stomach was now rumbling in hunger after practically an 18-hour fast at that point. The only thing on my mind now was how badly I couldn't wait to get home and figure out what to eat for dinner. Finally, making it to my destination, I approached my apartment breezeway and began to race up the stairs, eager to invite my roommate, Corey, to join me for a bite.

As I climbed the right side of the staircase to my top floor unit, I noticed a delivery man from Jimmy John's, coming down the stairs. A frown completely consumed his face, showing a look of pure disgust. Assuming this reaction was the result of an exchange he had with a customer, curiously I asked, "Hey, man, how's it going?" Anticipating a generic response, like "fine" or "good," to my surprise, he immediately responded, "Could be much better. Asshole upstairs isn't tipping." His response was so fluent and charged with emotion, almost as if he had been repeating it over and over in his head, waiting for someone to share it with. Naturally, I extended my best regards to him, and wishes that his day would only get better from here. I then continued my climb to my apartment. I opened my front door, eager to tell Corey about this encounter, and to my surprise, I found him in the living room, with a smile on his face from ear to ear, almost as if he were an eight-year-old child in a candy store. There he was, hugging his foot-long feast, when it all started to make sense. Hysterically, I pointed at him and cried out, "Oh, my God, you're the asshole that's not tipping?" Corey replied, "Hell no; what for? Handing me a pen?" Shaking my head, we laughed and continued to discuss the series of events that led up to my epiphany, all the while I placed a very similar order of my own to Jimmy John's, hoping I wouldn't meet the same scarred delivery man.

Now, was Corey wrong for not tipping the delivery driver? I mean, the guy did everything right. Right? Corey placed an order, and when it arrived, the order was exactly what he wanted. The delivery guy climbed all three flights of stairs to get to the top floor, and brought the food to our doorstep instead of telling Corey to come down and pick it up; not to mention his order arrived within 20 minutes of ordering it. This is the epitome of good customer service.

So, should Corey have left him a tip? Many of you would argue that yes, Corey should have compensated the delivery man for his service, and had it been you in a similar predicament, you would have done things differently. Respectfully, I disagree.

Now, I say this with the utmost respect for those in the service industry. As an almost shamefully habitual consumer, I recognize that servers receive far more scrutiny than they do the praise they deserve. However, contrary to any sentiment to the service industry, I think you can agree that Corey had a valid point. At what point was any additional payment warranted in this matter? Corey placed an order online to Jimmy John's, and practically spelled out exactly how he wanted his sandwich prepared. Then he agreed to pay the service charge for not only the sandwich but also for the delivery premium that is attached to every item delivered; not to mention, the biggest selling point that Jimmy John's has on all of its competition is the fact that its delivery time is freaky fast! Jimmy John's niche is its convenience. So when ordering from Jimmy John's, that hasty, front door service is exactly what Corey was paying for. Therefore, at what point was it warranted for Corey to pay anything additional beyond mere sympathy?

The driver is a great example of how many perceive customer service today. You treat customer service as a series of procedures that if executed properly it will appease the buyer, in hopes that they will prove to be a repeat buyer. Therefore, you spend so much time focusing on doing things right that you forget what is most important: how you make the customer feel. Jimmy John's flawlessly executed Corey's order, delivery time, and convenience. According to Jimmy John's standard, the service was perfect, but then when it came down to the one moment that actually mattered, all the driver did was pass Corey a pen and said, "Here, sign this." This cold, stale interaction alone feels just like any other familiar transaction you would encounter, where you sign a contract and receive a service—fair exchange. This is the most fundamental problem with customer service: It is solely and equally exchange.

We are a sophisticated people who are driven by results, especially in the leasing industry. You focus on what works and what is going to make money. So, by default, you establish a series of procedures that you execute consistently to make sure the customer is content with your service. The problem is, customer service without hospitality is merely a commercial transaction. When I buy Jimmy John's sandwiches, I expect them to come freaky fast. When I contract with Verizon, I expect to have reliable mobile phone service. If I order from Amazon Prime, I expect my order to be at my doorstep in 2 days. This level of customer service is a commodity; it is built into the product. The reason people are willing to pay premium rates is to receive this high level of customer service. Therefore, customer service is a fair exchange between buyer and seller. So, when the customer receives *good service*, it doesn't exceed their expectations; it does exactly what they paid for it to do.

Maya Angelou, *American poet,* said it best: *"People will forget what you said, people will forget what you did, but people will never forget how you made them feel."* The positive elicit feeling of inclusion, welcoming, and comfort that your lead feels on the other side of service—that's what they remember. This warm feeling of care, compassion, and sense of purpose is called hospitality. Hospitality is what people rant, rave, and leave reviews over—not customer service. When your lead walks into your community, they want to FEEL at home, not processed. It's not the perfect execution of a set of procedures that will impress them; that's already expected. The fundamental problem with why good service will only be good at best is because it will always simply be a fair exchange. It is what people expect, because that is what they are paying for.

We work in the hospitality industry, but too often, people focus on everything but being hospitable. This one dimensional mindset of customer service is what inspired our seventh Hitch Leasing Principle: *"What if fine isn't good enough… What if I want extraordinary?"* When it comes to a lead describing your community, you should never want to hear three, four-letter words, as they essentially have the same meaning: "Fuck!" Words like fine, okay, and good are the f-bombs of leasing, and all mean that your community is simply average at best. When you focus solely on providing *good* customer service, you will always only be good enough. Instead, focus on being hospitable, because when your concentration is on providing an experience that leaves your leads feeling good, that is when your service becomes extraordinary!

The Extra Mile Wins Hearts

Think for a moment. When was the last time you personally had an extraordinary customer experience? Meditate on that experience for a moment. Where were you at? What did it look like? Who were you with, if anyone at all? What made this experience stand out from the rest? Most importantly, how did it make you feel?

Still thinking about it? Don't be so hard on yourself if you can't think of one right away. Surprisingly, most struggle with this exercise. I had the opportunity to tune into a TED Talk a couple years back, discussing the phenomenon of memorable customer service, and have practiced this exercise in many of my leasing trainings since. Strikingly, an overwhelming percentage of people have a hard time remembering great customer experiences. Oddly enough, those same people, when asked to discuss a bad customer experience, were very easily able to remember a bad experience they had, and couldn't wait to tell their story.

There is a common customer service statistic that reads: People who receive great customer service, if they share at all, will likely only tell 5 other people about the service they received. On the contrary, people who receive bad customer service will, on average, tell 15 people or more about how bad of an experience they had. But why is that?

Why are people more inclined to dwell on and remember a bad experience opposed to a great experience? The answer is, as discussed prior, people don't remember what you say or do; they remember how you make them feel. When a customer enters any establishment, they have a clear expectation for the level of service they wish to have. If you go into Chick-fil-A, you expect to be met with hospitable service and enjoy a quality meal served quickly. It's just that simple. You get your chicken, and you go about your merry way. But what happens when that expectation isn't met? If you were to walk into that same Chick-fil-A, and they ran out of chicken, or the customer service representative was an asshole, you would probably flip shit!

Expectations are only good for one thing, and that is disappointment. Notice how, in the example above, when the need for chicken and good service was met, there was no real elation that came from that experience. Chick-fil-A met the customer's expectation; therefore, the customer was satisfied. However, on the contrary, where the expectation wasn't met, there was an immediate emotionally triggered response. It's hard for people to remember great customer service, because it is expected. In fact, there are studies that show that even for a client that has a flawless customer experience their first time visiting a restaurant, the statistical likelihood of them revisiting said restaurant is only about 40%. Why? Simply because the service only just met the customer's expectation—nothing more, nothing less.

We remember bad service because it is more visceral, and it triggers an emotional disposition that drives the urge for us to want to tell someone else about our experience. The customer will go above and beyond—move mountains—just to find the biggest name tag in the office to complain about a bad experience they've had. "I need to speak to the manager!" Then, when they don't get the response they want, they will leave a novel of a review on Yelp, Facebook, Google, and everywhere else they can get their hands on, just fill the emotional void they are facing.

I vividly remember an example of bad customer service I had experienced. I was travelling for a site visit, to Greenville, North Carolina. After a long day of travel, I still wanted to make sure to maximize the client's dollar, as well as my time with the team. Consequently, I went straight from the airport to the property, and stayed on-site until about 7pm. After a long day of trudging through TSA, travelling the turbulent skies, and employee training, naturally I was exhausted and ready to call it a night. Upon booking my travel, all my preferred Hilton hotel options were sold out, so I decided to try out the Best Western, as it was the closest accommodation to the property, and a more affordable option. Apprehensively, I walked into the hotel, and immediately, my insidious feeling of anxiousness was justified.

As I approached the reception desk, I heard a deep sigh, as if I had just interrupted the climax of a really good film. "Can I help you?" the receptionist asked, as I thought to myself, "Well, clearly, the grey and orange, Nautica, carry-on luggage I was dragging, along with the black leather laptop bag over my shoulder, would indicate that obviously I wanted to check in." However, recognizing that she may have been having a tough day, I responded, "Yes, I was hoping to check-in please." Sighing again, she now put down what looked to be a McRib from McDonald's, on the counter top, and proceeded to process my check-in. She went further to tell me that check out was at 11am on Thursday, and pointed me in the direction of my room. The interaction was cold and transient, and as I walked to my room, I immediately felt like I had burdened her. It wasn't until the next day that someone asked how I was doing and actually cared to hear my response.

I tell you this story simply to put it in perspective that the reason why it is hard to remember great customer service is because it is expected. You don't get any further elation from service that meets your expectations, because that is what you pay for. Bad customer service experiences, however, are more memorable because they make you FEEL bad. It is the emotional withdrawal elicited from either end of the spectrum that is what makes the experience memorable. The bad news is that people suck at customer service in the student housing space. The customer service standard is ridiculously low, and if you look hard enough in your respective market, you will surely see it. On the other hand, the good news is that there is a silver lining. Because the standards are so low, it makes for very minimal expectations from our leads. Therefore, if expectations are so low, a little hospitality can go a long way and truly distinguish you from your competition.

The late Zig Ziglar said, *"There are no traffic jams along the extra mile."* The idea of the extra mile being a lonely place is such a common idiom, yet so many have still not grasped the concept. If you continue to do what everyone else does, you will get what everyone else gets. But the moment that you decide to work a little bit harder, pay a little more attention to your leads, and focus a little more on the people instead of the outcome, you will begin to distinguish yourself from the white noise.

I remember, shortly after a tour training I hosted with my team, in Statesboro, GA, we quickly saw an immediate return. A student and her guarantor walked into the leasing office and requested to view a unit. Listening from the back office, I watched as one of our community assistants, Jalisa, fully embraced all of the tips from our training. Jalisa executed the customer greeting flawlessly. She then offered our guests coffee and refreshments, as she guided them to relax in the lobby couches, as she got to know them. She took the time to build rapport like this was a first date, and she genuinely wanted to know everything about them. Based on the level of laughter and comfort, you would've thought the leads were guests sitting in the middle of Jalisa's living room as her special guests. Finally, Jalisa perfectly painted the picture of the lead living in our community as if this was already their home. The guests were having the time of their lives, but then the unexpected happen. "Wait... I am going to stop you right here," uttered the guarantor. Jalisa's face was now full of confusion, and she was shocked at the reaction of the parent. "I'll just save you the time now," the guarantor continued. "You can keep doing the whole tour thing, but we are going to sign a lease here today. We have went to just about every community here in Statesboro, and you are the only place that made us feel at home."

You see, people are not looking for an apartment; they are looking for a place to call home away from home. It's like the saying: "Home is where the heart is." It is beyond the robust amenity package you have, and beyond the concessions you may be offering. Your leads expect to be offered all of these things when they walk in your door for a tour. But what they aren't expecting is for people to truly care about their well-being and make them feel like part of a community. Merely going the extra mile to make your lead feel at home is the easiest way to guarantee they soon will be. This is the type of hospitality that is memorable, and the type worth ranting, raving, and leaving reviews about!

Good Hospitality = Good Review

People do not go above and beyond to tell others about average experiences. Reviews are another example of leasing that shares striking similarities with dating. If you go on a mediocre first date, chances are you probably won't be too eager to call the person back, nor would you run to tell all your friends about how average of a time you had. Chances are, this date will be just another one of those things you did that one time. On the other hand, imagine if you had a horrible experience on that first date—one so bad that you weren't even able to see it through to the end. You get up to leave the date, and the very first thing you do is pull out your phone and call your best friend to pick you up. Before your friend can even ask how the date went, you blurt out, "This guy is a complete asshole. Please come get me, and I'll tell you all about it." Eventually, after telling just one friend, this horrible experience has become the brunt of a running joke that fuels every girl's night for the next month or so. Now everyone in your friend's group would know about this joke of a date before it finally blows over. Naturally, we can't wait to tell people about those bad stories. Interestingly, a good first date would likely only be told to a close circle of your friends, which wouldn't come close to the number of people you would tell the bad story. What's worse is that the poor guy on the other side of the date may never know just how good his first impression was, unless the lucky bastard gets a second chance, and this time has the guts to ask you straight up.

What if there was a way for that gentleman to see how well he had been graded on that first date? What if there was technology that allowed him to see, on a scale of 1–5, how well he performed? On the contrary, had the lady been able to view the dating average of the first guy, do you think she would have made the decision to give him a try? Would she have wasted her time if she knew he was an asshole who only had a 2-point rating?

Unfortunately, I am not sure that this technology exists

in the conventional dating world just yet, but if not, here is a free app idea for the next Whitney Wolfe. You're welcome. However, as for the leasing world, this is a technology that is alive and thriving. This is called your online reputation. Just about 90% of all consumers Google and utilize online reviews at some point in their apartment search before making a commitment to any particular community. That means that 9 out of every 10 prospects that you have worked diligently to get into your ecosystem, has already prejudged you before ever getting a chance to know your product. It's the same as what I do every time I consider watching a movie. If I see a trailer for a movie that looks even remotely interesting, no matter how awesome I think the trailer looks, the first thing I do is pull up Rotten Tomatoes to help confirm whether or not I should even waste my time on it. Unless the movie comes highly recommended from a friend, anything below a 70%, I won't give the time of day. This is how your communities work. Over 70% of prospective buyers believe that any star rating 3.5 and below just isn't good enough; thus, it results in you losing a lot of potential leads, without even having a chance to salvage them.

The issue is that too many of you are letting your consumers Rotten Tomato your community, and you're okay with it. And if you're not okay, you don't make increasing your reputation as much of a priority as you should. The harsh reality is that we live in a review-driven economy where you are constantly judged on a 5-point scale to determine your property's worth from just about every prospect that is even remotely considering your community. If the only effort being put in to increasing your score is the static bandit sign in front of the leasing office, saying, "Tell us how we're doing," or the flyers on the leasing desk, in acrylic frames, encouraging your residents to leave you a positive review, then you are in trouble. When your lead walks in and see tons of flyers and propaganda urging them to leave a review, it discredits the genuine nature of a review itself, and begs for an ingenuous response. Your leads can see that it is just another way to boost your reputation, and their review will simply be another spoke in the wheel of your sales ploy to lease up your community.

I agree that urging your customers and residents to leave reviews is wildly important. In fact, the whole point of this rant is to implore you to make increasing the amount of reviews you get on a weekly basis equal to, if not more significant than, many of the other goal metrics you set for your team. However, you have to be conscious of the methods you use to capture such reviews, and the quality of the review your efforts will yield. For instance, we all know that the easiest way to pull students' responses is to incentivize them. "Leave us a review, and get put into a raffle for a new pair of Air Pods," or whatever the new technology is by the time you read this book. Indeed, you will find some success doing this. Eager to win the raffle, your leads will surely leave you a 5-star review. This is great for your star rating, but when your lead is solely making a review with the intent of gaining a prize on the other end of the deal, it dilutes the quality of the review, because it is tainted by personal gain.

We all know that the best reviews are not those that read "great community with cool amenities." Those do very little for onlooking prospects. The best reviews are well thought out and include specific reviews where the customer articulates how the leasing agent was able to see a problem, solve the problem, and go the extra mile to be hospitable to the guest. A review showing that this experience was beyond simply a customer transaction, shows that the agent actually showed they cared. The quality of a review is defined by the customer's testimonial. Sure, the number one thing students look at when evaluating a community is your star rating. On a 5-point scale, how do you stack up? Then, immediately after, they review the volume of reviews, and the date the most recent reviews were made, to gauge your relevance. As studies show, about 77% of consumers believe that reviews over 90 days old are irrelevant. But once that one-minute long vetting period is complete, the content of the review is where students spend the majority of their time, reviewing other's experiences and how managers responded accordingly.

As the very first person to introduce a lead into your community's ecosystem, it is amazing the amount of influence you can have over the quality of their experience; thus, their aptitude is to leave you a good review. This is especially the case if you helped walk them through the entire leasing processes and found them their dream apartment. At this point, you are their hero! They had a problem of not knowing where they were going to live, and you swooped in to save the day. Your lead is on Cloud 9 at this point. Use this as an opportunity to ask for a review. Ask your lead to do you a favor as you have just done for them, and not only will they leave you a good review, they will provide a novel of a testimony to share with the world.

This is the key to maximizing SEO. Google is obsessed with new micro content, so the more you encourage your leads to leave reviews, the more you feed the Google algorithm, which gives you more visibility and drives more traffic to your community. This is why hospitality is so important. Make your lead feel at home, make them feel comfortable, let them know that you care, and when you see a problem, provide a solution. Then, when they are at the climax of what seems to be a situation so perfect it's cinematic, ask for the review. Do it right then and there, because at that point, you have won your lead's heart, and you deserve to boast your 100% score on Student Housing's Rotten Tomatoes.

Secure the Bag

So, we all understand the significance of getting more reviews, right? The more reviews you get, the greater optimization ranking your property has. The greater your ranking, the more visibility your website gets. With more visibility comes traffic, and with more traffic, comes more leases. That all seems simple enough, right? Your online reputation is your property's real first impression on a lead, and the way you present yourself can make the difference between an online inquiry converting to a tour or reverting to a loss. I am confident by now that you understand the impact a customer review has on your property. What seems to be lacking is the knowledge as to how to get more reviews to peacock your community's brand.

Increasing your online reputation is one of most important things you can do to lease up your community, yet interestingly, it is often one of the more frequently overlooked. Most likely, this is due to the perceived difficulty your team has on getting more reviews, which outweighs their ambition to do so. It's like what Thomas Edison said: *"Opportunity is missed by most because it is dressed in overalls and looks like hard work."* It's not the task itself that is actually so bewildering; it's simply the idea that it looks like more work than you are interested in putting in. You think that because you gave an excellent tour, and you provided good customer service, that your lead is going to leave a positive review. I mean, that's the right thing to do, right? Wrong! Only about 30% of students leave reviews at their respective communities. Why? Because the other 70% have never been asked to do so. Getting more reviews is not rocket science. In fact, it's a lot easier than you think. The easiest way to get a review is to ask for the review.

I remember, vividly, when I was on the other side of a

phenomenal customer experience, when my fiancé and I went out to eat at a restaurant for the first time. I would boast how amazing the service was, but honestly, it was beyond just the service. It was more about how hospitable our server was, and how he made us feel, that made this experience so memorable.

It was our very first New Year's Day in the city with no limits, Houston, Texas. After spending the entire week prior, entertaining friends from out of town, our pantry was now bare, and our energy at an all-time low. It was this lack of motivation that compelled us to want to dine out in the first place, and little did we know that it would be the first really great decision we made of 2019.

We perused the internet to find an accommodation that was appetizing and equally convenient for us to dine in and celebrate the holiday. However, we met failure, over and over again, with just about every restaurant in Houston labelled "Closed on New Year's Day." Then, my fiancé uttered the words, "Would you be game for Pakistani/Indian food?" Hesitant, as I had only eaten such cuisine a handful of times prior, I responded, "I'd be down, but first, what's the name of the place?" Aga's Restaurant and Catering was the name she disclosed, and immediately, the first thing I did was type the restaurant name into Google to vet the reviews. To my surprise, Aga's online rating boasted a whopping 4.9 stars out of 5, with over 4,000 reviews! Not to mention, it was the only option we could find that was open during the holiday. So, after analyzing all the kind words from previous Aga's customers, it would go without question that we would give this place a try.

When we arrived at the restaurant, we were immediately met with an almost euphoric energy. It was nothing tangible or anything that could be seen with the naked eye, but it was ever present, and felt by everyone. It was the same type of feeling you get from a family reunion, or when you and all your loved ones gather for Thanksgiving dinner. It seemed as if everyone enjoyed being in the presence of all their loved ones; but interestingly, they were all complete strangers to one another. Everyone felt welcomed, and we would soon meet the same treatment.

At first, the wait time seemed intimidating. When we arrived, the line started at the reception desk at the far end of the lobby, and extended all the way out the entrance door and alongside the building's exterior. In any conventional situation, we would have reconsidered our options, but my fiancé and I agreed that the experience would be worth the wait, and we already made the commute—so what the hell; we might as well see it through. To our surprise, it only took about 10 minutes before we were at the front of what seemed to be an endless line. It was not long before the manager, Sufiyan, came to greet my fiancé and me. He approached us with his wing span stretching from wall to wall, and a smile equal in length. Sufiyan reached out to shake my hand and pulled me in for a hug simultaneously. It was almost as if we were long lost friends coming together for our 10-year reunion.

He then greeted my fiancé with the same enthusiasm, but this time shaking her hand with his right on the bottom and his left gracing the top, as he bowed his head as if she was royalty. This was all before we finally sat to order our meal.

Now, sitting at our booth, Sufiyan recognized we were comfortable, and asked, "Is this your first time at Aga's?" When we confirmed, a look of pure bliss rushed across his face as if it was the best news he had heard all day. Then, as our intended server approached the table, Sufiyan interjected and insisted that he would take care of us during our stay. After taking our drink orders and suggestions for starters, he left us to explore the menu. Then, in just a few moments, Sufiyan returned with our appetizers and beverages of choice. He asked, "So, do you have any questions about the menu?" My fiancé expressed her interest in the curry chicken, while I inquired about the curry goat, but neither of us was sure exactly which of the many options to choose from. After Sufiyan asked a few more questions to get to know each of us and our desired pallets, he confidently confirmed, "Don't worry; I know just the thing."

Our order now in, we decided to go to the restroom to freshen up before our meal. It wasn't more than 7 minutes after we returned to our seats that our meal was hot and ready, waiting for us to enjoy. The presentation of the meal was top tier and definitely social media picture worthy, because, you know, Snapchat eats first. The flavor of the food was unlike anything we had ever had before, but everything we imagined heaven would taste like. The service was overwhelmingly immaculate, as I couldn't even drink my water a quarter of the way down before it miraculously was full again, all the way to the streamlined process of collecting payment, by bringing an iPad to the table for us to review the receipt and make payment all in one transaction. This experience was arguably one of the best restaurant experiences we had, but it was not over yet.

As if we were not already high enough on the Aga's experience, Sufiyan returned with another slice of heaven. "For our special guests," Sufiyan stated, as he delivered a complimentary dessert to the center of our table. My fiancé's hands rose up to cover her face in shock as she cried out, "Oh, my God, I feel like a princess." The dessert was called Gajar Halwa, with ice cream, which I soon learned was carrots cooked in milk, and seasoned to perfection, then garnished with pistachio flavored ice cream. By just reading the ingredients, this probably would not have been my first dessert choice on the menu either, but after trying it, I cannot see myself ordering anything else. It was delicious!!!

At this point, Sufiyan had outdone himself. He executed perfect hospitality, and he had us at an all-time high, when this happened … After finishing our delectable treat, Sufiyan approached our table to receive our used dishes. At this moment, he proceeded to ask, "So, how was your very first Aga's experience?" Little did he know that he had opened the flood gates. We ranted on about how amazing the food was, how awesome the service was, and most importantly, how much of a pleasure it was to have worked with him specifically. Then my fiancé asked, "Why were you so pleasant to us?" This is where it happened, the moment Sufiyan had been waiting for. Immediately, he straightened his posture, and his face drained of all emotion, almost as if he was approaching a podium ready to deliver his Oscar winning speech.

"My goal is to offer an amazing experience to everyone who walks into Aga's," Sufiyan began. "I want to make everyone who I have the pleasure of serving, feel the same way as my mother, my father, my sister, or my brother would feel, if they were to come eat at my restaurant. My goal is to make you feel like family." Touched by his ambition and altruism, we assured him his mission was accomplished. He then did not hesitate when he said, "I am so happy that you enjoyed yourself today. If I could ask one favor, it would mean the world to me." Nonchalantly, we replied, "Absolutely... anything!" as we signaled him to proceed with his request. "So much of our business is based on customer reviews. It would mean so much to me if you could leave us a review on Google about your experience. Let us know how you felt the service was, and if you enjoyed the food, and if you could also mention that I helped you, it would mean a lot to me." I realized in that moment that the initial look of excitement that had filled Sufiyan's face was in fact a look of opportunity. He was excited about serving a new customer, not because he would get a nice tip on the other side, but because he could offer an amazing experience, and in exchange, get a positive review. And he was right.

There is no secret sauce or special shortcut as to why Aga's has over 4,000 reviews, and at the time, maintains a 4.9 star rating on Google. They are confident in their ability to provide amazing service, and much like any of us who are passionate about what we do, they want to know how well they are doing. The only difference with Sufiyan and the rest of the Aga's team is that they just aren't shy to ask, and they do so consistently.

There was nothing earth shattering about what Sufiyan did, but his methods, however, are worth dissecting. First and foremost, upon meeting Sufiyan, the pure hospitality emanated through him like a pheromone bleeding through his pores. He most literally greeted us with open arms, making us feel welcomed and comfortable. He was also able to establish a sense of trust and familiarity with us, early on in our encounter. Then he built rapport with us, and recognized that this moment was our very first impression with Aga's. Recognizing that he was our very first encounter with his restaurant, and the influence he now had on us, he decided to change their standard procedure. Instead of having another person from the wait staff come to serve after he greeted us, he instead told his team that he would take care of us from start to finish, as the sense of security we already had with him could really have an impact on our first experience.

Sufiyan then figured out exactly what we wanted and tailored his suggestions to our pallet specifically. The team executed perfect customer service and made sure that we had a phenomenal experience by simply asking if we had enjoyed ourselves. Then, at that very moment, he found the sweet spot. While we were at the climax of our outing, he asked for the review. This is one of the most important moments to point out: timing is everything. Much like we like our meals fresh out of the oven, piping hot, so do we our reviews. You want to catch your lead at the peak of their experience. That way, the pure bliss that they are feeling will pour out in the testimonial they leave.

Now let's pay respects to how he asked for the review. Sufiyan opened by telling us what his goal was in our encounter together. He told us that his intent was to make us feel like family by the end our time spent together. He then revisited the idea that he accomplished his goal, by saying, "I am so happy that you enjoyed yourself today," which further incepted the idea that our time spent was pleasant. This moment alone allowed us to continue to ride the wave of this amazing experience and relive all the high points in our mind, which would make great content for our review.

Finally, once he cunningly reminded us how much joy Aga's was able to bring into our life, he asked us to do a simple favor for him that would mean the world to his business—leave a review. This is reciprocity at its finest. But he didn't just ask for any review; he was very specific in where he would like us to leave the review, and what he wanted us to discuss when writing it. This is wildly important to remember. Placement and content are major factors in monitoring the quality of a review. Find your niche platform, and send people to it to leave you a review. My personal advice would be to over index on Google. However, whether your demand is on Facebook, Yelp, etc., recommend your leads to leave their review on your desired platform. You cannot just hope that they will go to the medium you had in mind—guide them. Then shamelessly coach them on what you would like them to discuss. Remember, it is these testimonials that make for the best reviews.

Increasing your reviews is not brain surgery; it's really a lot simpler than you make it out to be. Continue to execute phenomenal customer service. Make sure that you care about your lead enough to deploy excellent hospitality that will make for an experience worth talking about. Then, when you find the sweet spot, don't be afraid to ask for the review.

And Then… You Ask for the Renewal

There is a reason as to why we are discussing renewals in the same conversation as hospitality and customer service. The concepts of customer service, hospitality, and retention go hand in hand, but at some point, these lines have been blurred.

Somewhere along the line, we have been confused and misguided by what is defined as *renewal season*—renewal season, as in the 2.5 months you dedicate to wining and dining your residents to remind them how much fun it is to live in your community; the 2.5 months before students check out for the holidays, where you roll out your lowest incentives and greatest concessions to entice your current customers to repurchase by renewing their leases for the upcoming fall. The 2.5 months— October, November, and half of December—where you finally show your residents that you actually give a shit about them; and why? Is it because you actually do care, or is it so that you can get another lease closer to budgeted pre-lease occupancy? I would argue the latter.

We've got it all backwards. Renewal season is far more than 2.5 months of honey dicking your residents just to get them to renew their lease before you are back to treating them like shit again. Renewal season is 25 hours a day, 8 days a week, 366 days a year. Renewal season starts the moment you say hello to your lead, and lasts throughout every experience you cast from that point on. Renewal season is year round, not just October. October is the final lap after a year-long marathon of busting your ass. October is simply the time that you watch the fruit of your labor come to fruition. October is the time to allow your residents to show their appreciation and gratitude for the work you have put in all year to make for an unparalleled experience. To have a successful renewal season, it requires a steadfast obsession with the year round renewal process, and that process is defined by the constant investment in your people. Resident retention is not a 2.5-month sprint of pretending you care. It is a 12-month marathon of showing that you do care, and demonstrating that appreciation through a value-conscious web of hospitality.

The reason why renewal season is typically such a grand gesture is because the overall acquisitions concept of leasing is exciting. The rush you get when you send out a mass email that actually pulls response is addicting. You send an email that says, "Because of who you are, we want to offer you this special rate," and it works. This is exciting! The chase of acquiring leases for the upcoming year is exhilarating. So when *renewal season* comes, it's a big deal! You host grand resident appreciation weeks, full of free breakfast on the go events, free food in the clubhouse, VIP parties, and even pet parades to make sure your furry residents feel at home too. Indeed, these events are awesome! However, the problem is, when you're only hosting these extravagant events and selfless gestures when it is time to ask your residents to renew their lease, it becomes less of hospitality and more of a commodity.

The truth is, the property that can maintain the greatest degree of humanity, will experience the least amount of turnover, but when your customer service becomes solely transactional, focusing on humanity is the last thing that you are doing. This is where hospitality kicks in. Hospitality, at its very core, is recognizing that we are all humans first, and taking the time to acknowledge each other's humanity. That's what your students are looking for. When a student goes on the market looking for a new home, they are looking for exactly that—a home. They want to find something closest to their heart, and let's face it; in order to get ahead in student housing, you have to be willing to touch many hearts. Students want to live somewhere effortlessly, without compromising their standard of living. They want to find a one-stop shop, where they can have everything conveniently in one place—not simply in the sense of amenities, but in the perks that cannot be monetized—the all-encompassing value that would only come second to what would be found under a mom's roof. That's the amenity package worth sticking around for.

The community who will win is one who weaves an all-inclusive value web of hospitality for their residents; the community who simply imagines the journey of the college student, and cultivates a culture of investing in that voyage, proactively paying attention to your resident's values, and making them your own, whether that be the students social life and their affiliation with student organizations, or an international student's cultural values and their yearning to learn more about the American ways. It could be a student's need for recreation and having a safe, controlled place to fill that void, or more focus on education and having the proper resources to help get through their schooling. As a property manager, think to yourself: How can you cultivate a culture centered on the needs of your residents? Sometimes that need is simply having someone accessible that can listen to them voice a problem that at the time seems almost apocalyptic. Merely providing genuine consul in such an event can make a world of difference. The fact of the matter is, this is where the value lies—identifying the key values that mean the most to your residents, and investing in those consistently.

That is how you win, not by throwing in the kitchen sink during renewal season. The truth is that the *wow factor* of your community amenities have a short shelf life. Similarly, the concessions and promotions you offer only hold so much weight before they lose value. The true value that you can cast is in the intangibles, the value only found in the investment you make in your people. That's what makes your residents renew.

At the end of the day, the major takeaway is this: If you want to renew more of your residents, you must first add more value to your resident. If you want to add value to your residents, you must first value your residents. Show your residents that you value them, and not just during *renewal season* but year round. Live in a world of hospitality. Invest in making their experience one worth telling the world about. At the end of the day, people live to feel connections. If you don't believe me, do me a favor and do a small experiment around your office. Find all your students, in your office, with a Mac Book. Then host a small empirical observation of how many of them have stickers on the lap top. Then look and see how many of those stickers cover the half bitten apple on the back ... I'm willing to bet none of them do—and why? Because they identify with that brand. They feel a connection with Apple so profound that they want the world to see it. If you can emulate a connection with your residents like they have with Apple, there will be no amenity in the world that can sway your resident to move. Not convinced yet? Go ask one of your leasing agents to convert to a Samsung phone.

I bet they will laugh in your face.

When it comes to renewing your residents, too often, people focus their energy primarily on the product, so much so that they forget what is most important, which is the process. The process is the effort that is put in year round to take care of your people. That's it: The x factor is always people. And how you take care of your people is going to determine how many of them you will retain. Hospitality is the number one amenity your community has; everything else is simply a novelty. October, for some, will be the start of their renewal season, when they finally take the time to appreciate their residents. But for you, October is going to be the start of your victory lap, after a year-long marathon of hospitality.

You just have to be willing to put in the work.

CHAPTER 8

RELeasing

Hitch Leasing Principle on Just Work

"Basic Principles ... There Are None"

Leasing is simple. I won't dare to say it is easy, because if that were the case, everyone would lease up. I say *simple* in the sense that there is no secret sauce. Student housing is a very complex topic that may vary in each respective market. However, no matter where you are, the leasing fundamentals remain the same. If you want to be successful in student housing, you simply have to be willing to put in the work. Put your nose to the ground, and grind your way to the top. There are no shortcuts or cheat codes to fast track the process. Leasing requires pure grit, hard work, empathy, and altruism.

Remember, as long as you work hard to make sure

your people's lives are okay, at the end of the leasing season, your pre-lease occupancy will always be okay. I truly believe that. Remember, the goal is not to get to 100% occupancy; the goal is the manager or the leasing agent that you become in the process of getting there. It's all about the process, and the process is the people, whether that be hiring the right people, who love the grind and invest in your team, or recognizing the humanity of your leads, and investing in their living experience. Either way, your investment should always be in people, as I can guarantee that investment alone will pay in dividends.

Therefore, I will leave you with our final Hitch Leasing Principle, which is, *"Basic principles... there are none."*

You just have to work!

So get up, get to work, and start **RE**leasing today like you never leased before. Because once you apply these principles to your daily practice I guarantee you will never look at leasing the same way again.

Acknowledgements

Much like they say it takes a village to raise a child, the same idea applies when fully manifesting a thought that grows into a book. With this being my first written title, the journey alone took me on an emotional roller coaster — from long nights where, if sleep happened at all, I would wake up periodically throughout to jot down thoughts and analogies to use later as content, to early mornings where I would wake up at 4:15am and regurgitate my ideas on paper. However, no matter how vivid the idea, or how ambitious the thought, the following people truly made an impact in helping bring this dream to life, and for that, I am thankful. To the people that don't make it to this page, they will know this book to be written by one, but in actuality, this dream was manifested by many, and to you all, I am eternally grateful.

My Family

Eumaymah Shabazz – My beautiful and equally brilliant wife to be: For all the early morning TED talks I preached to you about leasing, inadvertently you helped refine those thoughts and bring them to fruition. You make me feel like I can take over the world, because I know if I tried, you would be right there by my side, supporting me every minute of the way. You bought me my journal to house my most elaborate ideas, you were my editor before the editor, and you were my one reason WHY I needed to finish this book, amongst the many "why nots." You deserve all the credit in the world for this book. Words cannot express my gratitude enough, so instead, I'll just say, I love you.

Satori Butler – Thank you for always believing in your ever ambitious big brother, and constantly supporting my wildest ideas, no matter how farfetched they were. You constantly held me accountable from literally the beginning to the end of me writing this book. Both literally and metaphorically, you were my motivation to endure through the storm that comes with writing a book. You helped me see the purpose in all the pain, as well as the struggles I endured, and for that, I am forever thankful. I love you, little sis.

Willie Butler Sr. – My father, for some wild reason, believes in me so much, he thinks of me as supernatural. Thank you for your unconditional support. Thank you for always challenging me to fully think beyond the limits of my own subjectivity and have a more objective frame of mind; not to mention that your constant reminder that this book was written by me, not for me, really changed my approach as I tailored my message. Your persistent encouragement kept me moving forward, and I appreciate every minute of your support. Thank you, and I love you.

Lydell Moore – My big brother and greatest role model: Growing up, you showed that striving for more was always within reach. Being the first of us to make it out of our neighborhood and off to college made me believe that I am capable of a lot more. That same ambition that you instilled in me, encouraged the discipline to write this book. Thank you for paving the way for all of us. I hope that one day we will be able to return the favor.

Lisa Delacruz – My wonderful big sister: Thank you for your unadulterated selflessness. You took me in as your little brother, looked after me, and always gave without expectation of anything in return. You have always supported me with true empathy and care for my well-being. It is through you that I have learned to appreciate the concept of empathy, which is the foundation for just about every lesson in this book. Thank you for always being there for me. I love you!

Stephanie Moore – My beautiful niece, you have and will always be my role model. Why? Because I look up to the passion you have for everything you do at such a young age. I admire your willingness to speak your mind despite popular opinion of those around you. You have the ambition to push yourself to heights that no typical 13-year-old ever should; not to mention your unparalleled strength to overcome all the major hurdles you have had to endure recently. Your resilience has inspired me to persist through the struggles of completing this book. Thank you for being my role model! I love you.

Antwyn Butler – I wish I could look up to someone the way you always looked up to me, for always thinking your uncle to be as strong as one of the Avengers, and always wanting to be just like me. You hold me accountable to be the best I can be, so I can encourage you to do the same. You encourage me to be a servant leader, and it is in that leadership I have been able to write this book. I hope one day you will read it and still think of me with such esteem.

Rory Boone – Your unprecedented hustle and drive is unmatched by anyone else that I know. Holidays consist of a meal, then back to the grind. Weekends are days on instead of days off. You inspire me to grind equally as hard. The very core of this book is built on the hustle and work, two things that you possess and I admire.

Tim Dietrick – My big brother that never fails to be there for me: No matter how old I get, you still look after me like I'm the same snotty-nosed kid back in High Point, West Seattle. You still pour nuggets of wisdom into me, and constantly cheer me on. It's this level of support and buy-in that helps motivate me to support and uplift my teams. You inspired me to write this book.

Employers and Colleagues

Ryan McGrath – Thank you for your investment in me. I still remember your call, expressing how bright of a future I have with your company. Thank you for believing in my abilities and investing in my career. I am forever grateful for everything you have invested in me, and for the chances you have taken on me. It is because of your investment in me that I have the knowledge and bandwidth to write this book.

Jason Fort – Thank you for truly being a role model, inside and outside the office. Thank you for showing me that no one is above the work, and that work itself is the only secret sauce. I've never met someone that possesses so much altruism that it almost literally seeps through their pores. The passion that you have for investing in your people shows in every word you speak, every step you take, and every breath you breathe. Your passion inspires me to be passionate about my craft, and thus, it encouraged me to write this book. Thank you for just being you and believing in me.

Mindy Brake – You call me your hero, but it is in fact the complete opposite. Thank you for not only being the best general manager any hard-headed, overly ambitious, leasing manager could ask for, but also for being the best role model I never knew I needed. That day, back in Cheney, WA, I knew we were expecting a new GM, but I didn't know I was getting a new member of my family. You never budged in your belief in me, and you always seem to support me even in my wildest ventures. You are simply the best. Your unwavering support and constant endorsements gave me the confidence to not only excel in student housing but to become a better person overall. Thank you Mama Mindy!

Saad Arij – Now, we all know how much you like to look at yourself, but secretly, what I admire about you most is your ability to look at everyone else. You always look for the best in your people, and you don't hesitate to give credit when it's due. You consistently endorse my strengths and publicly celebrate them; however, you don't hesitate to point out room for improvement, and challenge me to be the best version of me. Your servantship inspired and helped refine my perspective for investing in my teams the way you have for me. Thank you for being a great leader, but more so for becoming my brother.

Alex Abernathy – I still remember the moment that you walked into my first leasing trailer as a lease up specialist. I was super excited to show it off for the progress we made, but you didn't share the same excitement. In fact, your exact words were *"This looks ghetto."* In that moment and many more after you showed me the value of paying attention to the small details and always putting my best foot forward. Not to mention I've never shared a dull moment around you. Thank you for taking a shot on me with your New Development team and believing in me every moment since.

Allison Park – You always manage to see the best in me and support me in everything I aim to achieve. You have always had my back. Your optimistic spirit and contagious personality make it easy to want to be around you, and even easier to learn from you. I learned so much from you in our short time working with one another. Although it was short-lived, it will never be taken for granted. Your ability to always praise the good in me gave me the confidence to want to share this book with the world.

Thank you for being you. You are very much appreciated.

Corey Franklin – Never would I have ever guessed that a relationship that started freshman year of college would manifest into not only a true brotherhood, but us also working side by side in our careers. You were my partner in crime during our Michigan adventures, and every day since. Our girlfriends get mad because we get on the phone and talk for hours about life, love, property management, and everything else that comes to mind. My roommate, leasing manager, fellow RLTD, etc., but most importantly, my brother: Thank you for matching my ambition and love for the process. Your hunger helped encourage me to write this book.

Regional Leasing and Training Director Team – Thank you, all, for always challenging me to be the best version of myself. The endless support and brainstorming think tanks truly make it that much easier to find a way in student housing, where it otherwise seems like there is none. Thank you to you all: Anna Long, Emily Nelson, Kate Villines, Rosalie Albano, Ashley Malick, Jared Winn, Khalil Hall, Shayna Delaney, Callie Bryant, Jenny Stagner, Maggie Taylor, Shelby Sanders, Chad Hall, Jessica Mancuso, Maggie Freeland, Trent Martin, Corey Franklin, Kathleen Lines, Randi Rowland, Debra Baldacci, Kate McKeehan, Rebecca Capek

Early Career Influences

Sylvester Brandon – Thank you for being a mentor, role model, and a friend throughout my property management career; not to mention the fact that you took a shot on me in the first place, and vouched for me every moment since. I appreciate everything you have invested in my success. Without you taking a chance on me, neither this book nor my student housing career would have ever been possible.

Kevin Sealy – I still reminisce on our last Campus Crest 100% club trip to Puerto Vallarta, Mexico. I vividly remember the moment where I pulled you into a circle of onlookers, and you led the crowd in a full-on fist pump frenzy. This moment, among many others, spoke to who you genuinely were as a person, beyond your title and how you valued team culture. Everything from the weekly motivational calls, to the yearly 100% club trips, you showed me the value of culture and authenticity in a workplace. Thank you for everything you instilled in me to help make me the student housing professional I am today.

Amanda Stewart – Your cheerleader spirit and ambition for marketing is intoxicating and would bleed through our weekly calls. It was your eager spirit and unadulterated passion for marketing that encouraged my ambition to lease today like there is no tomorrow. Thanks for all the great ideas and the push to always be better. You inspired my hunger for leasing that I have today.

Mike Meehl – Thank you for believing I had the potential to grow in my career even before I did. I still have the first two books you bought me, *First Break All the Rules,* and *Strengths Finder 2.0.* You told me to read them to refine my management skills, reflect on my greatest strengths, and apply that knowledge to create a property management resume of all my experiences, and then use that to navigate my future. I did exactly as you told me. Your investment in me, and those books, gave me the confidence to go out and write my own. Thank you for believing in me.

The Raymond Aaron Group

Lisa Browning (Editor) – Thank you for making me look and sound a lot smarter than I actually am.

Raymond Aaron – Thank you for publishing this title and giving me the opportunity to make this dream come true.

The Greats – I can't pretend like I created all of these ideas on my own; many were created by the endless amount of content I have consumed and applied along the way. A special shout out to Jason Fried and David Heinemeier Hannsson. Their book, *Rework,* greatly inspired this book and kicked me in the butt to get started on writing my own. Also, thank you, Ryan Holiday, Mark Manson, Gary Vancherchuks, Tony Robbins, John Maxwell, Les Brown, Inky Johnson, and many, many more who helped me articulate my thoughts and drive these points home. Your content has changed my life, and I hope mine can now do the same for others.

YOU – To all of you hungry and daring enough to read this book and embody the spirit of wanting more, I hope, in one way, shape, or form, this book was able to add value to your life, your habits, and your perspective, and as a result, your leasing. Thank you again for everything.

About the Author

WILLIAM BUTLER is student housing enthusiast from West Seattle, WA, who has since relocated to Houston, TX. Butler is a middle sibling of two older, twin brothers and one younger sister. His passion and specialty lies in Student Housing Leasing, Outreach, and Training. He is the author of the award winning book *Releasing* and currently works as the corporate Training Developer of the largest third-party property management company in the nation for student housing.

It all started back in 2009 when Butler began his career in student housing as Leasing Agent in Cheney, WA. After transferring to another university, he returned to his student housing alma mater as a Sales Manager, taking on what was perceived to be an almost impossible lease up. After suffering many defeats and enduring umpteen failures, as a culmination of all setbacks, Butler was able to develop a leasing recipe that would later offer a promising future. This recipe transformed the "impossible" task in Cheney, WA in to a repeated inductee into the 100% club year over year for the first time in history since its establishment 7 years prior. Butler found such success a number of times since, including leasing up 2 new development properties on either side of the country, in the same 2016-2017 leasing year.

Butler has been fortunate enough to influence aspiring managers in just about every region in the nation, only to find that many are suffering from the same torment that plagued him in his early property management career. It is this reality that has inspired Butler to live each day aiming to provide the much needed shift in perspective that many ambitious property managers need to **RELEASE** them from the chains of conventional thinking about apartment leasing.

The author is available for delivering keynote presentations to appropriate audiences. For inquiries and availability please contact the author directly at wbutler@releasingup.com

Lastly, if you were able to find value in this book in any capacity, please let the author know. Your feedback means more than you know. Please leave your testimonials on www.releasingup.com.